I0096704

www.ingramcontent.com/pod-product-compliance
Lightning Source LLC
Chambersburg PA
CBHW052023030426
42335CB00026B/3260

9 781958 250006

# MANY PLANETS ONE PEOPLE

## Quantum Fragments in the Multiverse
### Infinite worlds connecting infinite lives. Be the author of your own destiny

by Lyle Benjamin & You

"Imagine all the people
Sharing all the world"
— John Lennon

I am a dreamer. I can sleep for 20 minutes and enter my land of dreams in two minutes. And in my dreams, I experience many of the things as I do when I'm awake: Conversations, scenarios, ideas, business issues and solutions. And when I'm asleep, I've also read all types of printed material: Schematics, blueprints, magazines, fiction, and non-fiction books, to 30-pound illustrated bibles with resplendent colored stained glass panels (although bibles don't show up too often).

Over the years when I've shared my dreams with friends, family, and even doctors, I've been told they are rather unusual. So, sometime after my Covid headaches began, I decided to write down some of my dreams. What I saw. What was said. I wrote them down verbatim. I didn't embellish. I didn't invent dialogue.

The dreams are slices of lives. They are but fragments of a day and there is always more to the story than what meets the eye. And this is where it gets interesting …

We are all connected: One Planet One People. But what if it went beyond that? What if the dreams are the gateway to Many Planets One People, and you are the key to telling the rest of the story?

Welcome to **Quantum Fragments in the Multiverse** (QFM) where you — as a contributing author — get to continue the story and submit. We post it and people share their thoughts about your contribution to the multiverse in our on-line community. Out of one story many will follow as they stream in from all corners of the globe.

Illustrator and artist works are welcome. The highest-ranking authors and artists receive recognition and rewards including their work being published. Visit the **ONE** book on our App for more information on how to enter the multiverse. All are welcome: Authors, artists, readers, and listeners. QFM is designed to be a fun, interesting and entertaining way to connect people.

I look forward to meeting you there. Stay safe. Stay well. LB.

**Proceeds from QFM go to support One Planet One People
and Planned Acts of Kindness programs and initiatives.**

# Happy Mother's Day!

This Book is Dedicated to You, Mom, Because You
Have Always Been The ONE There for Me

Mom, Your Love & Kindness
throughout the Years
Has Meant the World to Me.

May Your Everyday
Be Blessed with
Peace & Happiness.

I Love You, Mom.
Your Son,

# MOTHER'S DAY & MORE
## HOW TO COLLABORATE WITH THE ONE BOOK & BE THE HERO

# Every Day is Mother's Day!
## Make It ONE that will be Cherished for a Lifetime

### Give The ONE Book to the One Person
in Your Life that Gave You Life & Loves You Like No Other

### Your Mom will be Surprised & Delighted When
She Sees Her Name on the Cover of The ONE Book

### Imagine Her Amazement When She Turns the Page and Discovers that
She's the ONE You Dedicated the Book to with Picture, Art & Words

### Your Mother will be Touched to Her Soul with Honor & Joy
Give Your Mom the Keepsake that Reminds Her of
Your Love for All Her Days to Come

THE BEST MOM
Happy Mother's Day

# WARNING!

**Use of this Book and Said Contents are Restricted**
to the following five groups of individuals:
Students, Employees, Owners, Retirees and the Unemployed
and the following five types of institutions:
Schools, Faith-Based Organizations, Non-Profit Organizations,
Companies, and Government Agencies

**STOP**

# DO NOT PROCEED!

**Unless You Possess the Following Characteristics & Behaviors:**

1. **Desire** to help others
2. **Determination** to make a positive impact in the lives of others
3. **Willingness to Learn** how to do things differently to achieve better results
4. **Action** exhibiting behaviors designed to achieve objectives

**HEROES ONLY**

# ENTER AT OWN RISK!

**Only If You Are Willing to Join the Quest to "Be The Hero!"**

## WHY A PRINT BOOK?
## ESPECIALLY WHEN YOU'RE ALL ABOUT BEING GREEN?

• Because print books can be easily shared with others in person, and we are all about connections and collaborations — building and strengthening relationships.
• Because print books can engage people just by their visibility.
• Because print books can exude warm and fuzzy feelings that you just can't get from a phone, tablet, or computer. Really. I mean, whoever heard of somebody curling up with a good computer?
• The print book is a fun interesting and exciting page turner to go through with your relationship partner, friend, family member or a group. You can reference the book to form a team or community group through our App and hold meetings where you go through the programs, discuss, and then break into action groups.
• The print book allows people to engage with you, just by you carrying it around where other people can see it.
• Print books can be held onto for years and their value easily passed on to others.
• Print books can avoid the expression, "Out of sight, out of mind."

## WHY IS THE FRONT COVER SO DEVOID OF INFORMATION?

Planned Acts of Kindness and One Planet One People Founder, Lyle Benjamin designed the cover of the ONE book to be stark, engaging, and impactful. Every time you encounter it, it's literally in your face with the message: This is nothing short of the fight for the survival of the human race.

When the ONE book is on the table and people see the cover for the first time, they are immediately intrigued, "What is that?" and want to pick it up to learn more.

Every time you pick up the book to read it, it's going to remind you of what's at stake If we don't take collaborative action.

When people see you reading the book, the back of the book is like a front cover. It's designed to give you all the information you need about what's contained in the book and who wrote it. This way you can be engaging literally dozens of people a day as you are carrying the book around and reading it in public places where they can now easily find the book on their own.

## WHY IS SO MUCH OF THE BOOK DONE IN COLOR
## WITHOUT MUCH EXPLANATORY TEXT?

The book pages themselves are designed to be both engaging and informative. Instead of just describing things, we do our best to show you how a program works and how you can work with that program.

Pages and spreads in the book are mini posters that can be enlarged to boost their visibility and engagement when posted.

## WHAT DO I DO WHEN I SEE SOMETHING I'M INTERESTED IN?

Engagement is as simple as entering the page number in the ONE book section in the PAK app and then following the prompts.

"What you're doing is great. I'm glad you're taking on this project. We definitely need it. We've become so, let's just call, divided in our country and when we are just talking being human beings, about solving problems we all share, it doesn't matter what side of the political spectrum you're on."

— **Jack Canfield,** Best Selling Author of "Chicken Soup for the Soul" and "The Success Principles"

"This is what the world needs now. We have been divided too long and collaboration is the path we need to take to if we are to achieve our goals. I am fully committed to supporting the programs of Planned Acts of Kindness and One Planet One People and am excited about my being of service with the organization."

— **Coumba Marenah,** Secretary of Education, Gambia Women's Council to the United Nations

"This is such a wonderful program, and such an important program. It's absolutely needed, and I encourage everyone to get involved!"

— **Trish Carr,** Business Success Coach and Co-Founder of the international Women's Prosperity Network

"I have witnessed the wonderful work that Lyle has done over the years and the absolute dedication he has to the Mission of providing Quality of Life to everyone regardless of race, religious, education or income. The community programs are truly life-changing."

— **Dr. Anthony Graham,** Educator, Assistant Director Eastern District of Wesleyan Churches

"In my position as a hedge fund manager, I get to see a great number of 'cutting edge' businesses looking to change the world. Upon analysis rarely do they live up to their claims. What Lyle has assembled is a collection of scalable programs that when combined together might just succeed as the "Go To" source to change the world."

— **Yvonne Gamble,** CEO/Founder SanPete Financial Group and FYNB (Financing Your NEXT Billion)

"I really see how this program can be a game changer. It's tremendously ambitious, but it has what it takes to make it happen."

— **Steve Harrison,** Bradley Communications. Founder of National Publicity Summit, Network & Radio/TV Interview Report (helped successfully launch "Rich Dad, Poor Dad" "Chicken Soup for the Soul" "Men Are From Mars ..."

"Planned Acts' programs are such a wonderful complement to our NGO's Mission, it's always a pleasure to work with Lyle and positive energy he brings to our meetings and events."

— **Sabita Geer,** Brahma Kumaris, NGO, India

## BOOKS:

"ONE" The Fight for Survival of the Human Race

"16 Things We All Can Do To Act Right &
Help Save The Planet!" Branded Special Editions

"The Working Dead" The Essential Survival Guide
How to Protect, Save & Invest for Yourself,
Your Family & Your Future

"Legacy LifeLines: Memorial Special Edition"
Keeping the Joy & Happiness of a Lost Loved One
Alive for You, Your Family & Generations to Come

"Legacy LifeLines: Memoirs Special Edition"
Keeping the Joy & Happiness of a Lost Loved One
Alive for You, Your Family & Generations to Come

## CAREER & FINANCIAL CERTIFICATION COURSES FOR QUALITY OF LIFE :

The PMOROS System
The Essential Project Management System
that Moves You from Management to Leadership

"Career Track Management"
8 Foundation Skills Certification Courses

"Money Matters Mastery"
Financial Literacy & Planning Course

"One Planet One People 4 Pillars Course"
Civility, Social Responsibility,
Volunteerism & Global Citizenship

# LYLE BENJAMIN

# ONE

## THE FIGHT FOR SURVIVAL OF THE HUMAN RACE

**PRESS**

**ESBN Press NY 2022**
**Entrepreneurs Sustainable Business Network**

# ONE
### The Fight for Survival of the Human Race

Copyright © 2022 by Lyle Benjamin. All rights reserved.

**ESBN Press**
20 East Broadway, 4th Fl
New York, NY 10002
1-212-213-0257

Individual Sales: This book is available through Amazon, bookstores, libraries, or can be ordered directly from our Apps or website: PlannedActs.Org.

Quantity Sales: Special discounts are available through sponsorship packages or quantity purchases by corporations, organizations, associations and others. For details, contact the "Special Sales Dept." by phone or through the ONE book section on our apps or websites.

Printed in the United States of America
*Library of Congress Cataloging-in-Publication Data*
is available from the publisher
ISBN 978-1-958250-00-6

Cover and Interior Design by Lyle Benjamin

Images: We use custom designed, public domain, and stock images and photographs. If you are the copyright holder of any image and would like to have it removed, please contact us in writing at the above address and we will remove it from all future editions. If you would like to receive free promotional copies of the ONE book with our gratitude, please let us know. Thank you.

**To Friends & Families From
All Corners of the World
Many of Whom I Have Yet To Meet**

*I Would Like To Offer A Special Thanks To
The Following People For Their
Support In Making This Book Happen:
Robert Adamo, Jacque Zoccoli, Alice Mok*

*Intern Trainees:
Richard Rodriquez, Pramath Kalelkar, Kyle Shattuck,
Xavier Polanco, Sean Murphy, Joanna Wang, Joey Wolf,
Steven Liu, Akash Patel*

*And to several lifelong friends that serve as
my inspiration every day:
Jon Anderson, Thomas Hewlett, Steve Werthman*

*And to my mom, Dolly, and my Uncle "The King" Ronnie —
who have always thought my endeavors were
ridiculously difficult and ambitious, especially for one person,
but whole-heartedly supported me none-the-less*

*And to God who has given me talents
and trials throughout my life that have helped
motivate me to be in service to others*

# PUBLISHER'S BOOK NOTES

This book is the product of years of program development by NPO founder, entrepreneur, and author, Lyle Benjamin. As you will see, the programs are unique in content not only in the world of non-profits, but companies and governments as well. From cover to cover, the ONE book's design reflects this innovation.

Benjamin's vision for the book is based on six factors: Outreach, Engagement, Inspiration, Education, Action and You. Everything in the book stems from this orientation including the decision to produce print books over digital e-books regardless of the expense. Likewise, the environmental cost of producing print books is dwarfed by the benefits readers like you can contribute in obtaining the 17 Sustainable Development Goals of the United Nations.

As you will see, we are all about the "Whys" — So here are a few more:
• Because print books can engage people just by their visibility.
• Because print books can be easily shared with others in person.
• Print books allow you to unplug and get more immersed in the content while being less subject to distractions: i.e., notifications, texts, cute kittens, etc.
• The ONE book is a fun, interesting and exciting page-turner to explore with your relationship partner, friend, family member or group. **Founder's note:** Form a community group through our App where you go through the programs, discuss, break into action groups, and share your successes with the world. You can even start a One Planet One People Club using the book as your Activity Guide!
• The print book allows people to engage with you, just by you carrying it around with you where other people can see it.
• Print books can be held onto for years and their value passed on to others.
• And, by no means, not the last or least reason: Because print books can engender warm and fuzzy feelings that you just can't get from an android phone, tablet, or computer. **Editor's note:** Since this mission is all about kindness, I pushed back on the author's intent to add an emoji here sticking out its tongue. **Author's note:** Whoever heard of someone curling up with a good computer?

Benjamin designed the cover of the ONE book to be stark, engaging, and impactful. When people see the front cover for the first time, they are going to be intrigued, "What is that?" They want to pick it up to learn more. Every time you encounter it, it's in your face with the message: This is nothing short of the fight for the survival of the human race. Every time you pick up the ONE book to read it, it's going to remind you of what's at stake If we don't take collaborative action.

When people see you reading the book, the back of the book is like a front cover. It's designed to give viewers all the information they need about what's contained in the book and who wrote it. You can be literally be outreaching to dozens of people a day as you carry the book around and read it in public places. You never know, it might end up being a great way to meet new friends.

Next, the ONE book pages themselves are designed to be mini-posters that are engaging and informative. Instead of just describing things, we do our best to show you how a program works and how you can work with that program. Engagement is as simple as entering the page number in the ONE book section in the PAK app and following the prompts.

# C O N T E N T S
## R = Read / A = Action

### Go to the ONE Book on the PAK App & Use Page Numbers to Take Action

# CONTENTS

# CONTENTS

## QUOTATIONS:

**Mahatma Gandhi • John F. Kennedy • Helen Keller • Cesar Chavez
Dr. Martin Luther King, Jr • Catherine Pulsifer • Tim Ferriss
Michael J. Fox • Steve Jobs • Oprah Winfrey • Jeffrey Sachs
Mother Teresa • Anne Frank • Pablo Picasso • Neil Armstrong • Spock
and John Lennon**

# FOUNDER'S NOTES

## HOW TO GET THE MOST FROM OUR PROGRAMS

### (EVEN IF YOUR FIRST THOUGHT IS TO PUT US IN DETENTION FOR BREAKING ALL THE RULES)

### Convention One:

Non-Profits should have one clear, concise message and vision in order to garner as much support as possible for their cause by not confusing people with multiple objectives.

The truth of the matter is that they have this approach to maximize their fundraising efforts because they view themselves in competition with other non-profits for dollars and this is the best approach to reach and capture players in their target market.

The problem with this path is that it perpetuates the fractional approach to solving the very problem the NPO is working to solve.

### Unconventional Approach One:

A much more effective approach would be to collaborate with organizations, educators, companies, and governments with similar objectives so that you're bringing more resources to bear on solving the problem.

Our approach to solving these global issues is to provide a collaborative system that brings similar institutions together as well as members of the other institutions, so that everyone is contributing to both finding the solutions to the problems and then taking action on solving the problems.

Main Program: Our Global Collaboration Think Tank is fully aligned with solving the United Nations Sustainable Development Goals for 2030.

### Convention Two:

Companies and organizations should only focus on issues that impact their area of operation, doing otherwise distracts them from their stated purpose and goals.

The problem with this line of thinking and behavior is that even if you are successful in your niche, you run the risk and the very real possibility that five years down the road you might not be conducting business as usual or have a business.

We are at the tipping point issues of climate change, pollution, pandemics, economic inequalities, food and water inequalities, health inequalities — where any one of these issues can overrun any business or organization on a local, national, or global scale.

If you think that you're not going to be affected because you're too small or too big — well, it may be one of your key suppliers that's affected and that essentially cuts your business or kills it. It may be that your customer base is adversely affected. It may be that your geography and your infrastructure is severely damaged. All these things are occurring today, but the real problem is when they escalate in the coming years will you have a job or a business to go to?

### Unconventional Approach Two:

The solution is to approach all the problems at the same time using the same collaborative system, so that you're not just reacting to problems, you are anticipating and preventing them from arising in the first place.

### Convention Three:

On a personal level, even after you buy into the multiple mission collaborative approach that we're putting forth, you want to know everything — and you mean everything — that goes into each of the Planned Acts and One Planet One People programs before you start sharing it with others.

### Unconventional Approach Three:

By the time that you learn everything, and you understand how to present it properly, the tipping points with already passed and so has quality of life for billions of people on the planet.

To put it simply, that's not your job and it's not effective use of your time and we have for every program that we put out we have the outreach and engagement side of the program and then we also have the business side of how we get our funding to make it scalable. And unless you're working on the business side there's no reason for you to know about it in detail.

A much more effective use of your time and to get you started very quickly is just to share the One Book and point out the programs that you believe they might be interested in — and don't even try to explain it. It's not your job, it's ours. When doing Outreach and engagement to your sphere. Just focus on making the connection. We do the heavy lifting and find out what their objectives are, and then match their objectives to the appropriate program(s).

Even if they ask you to explain the program to them, you should defer. We have the expertise, and we know how to customize each of the programs in order to provide better outcomes.

### Convention Four:

Another reason why you want to know everything in the first place is to help you target who you're going to share it with. You want to be absolutely certain it's a good fit before you share it.

### Unconventional Approach Four:

A better approach is to share it with as many people as you can and give them the opportunity to either recommend someone who might be interested or to get involved themselves. If they don't have the opportunity to see something, they never have a choice in the matter.

You don't want to be making peoples choices for them. Because you never know truly how busy someone is, how lazy they are, how overwhelmed they are, how too rich they are to be bothered, or too poor to be bothered — when they come across something that really resonates in their heart. When that happens busy people can make the time, lazy people can make the time, overwhelmed people can make the time, rich people and poor people alike can make the time.

Don't fall into the trap of making assumptions and being their gatekeeper. It's critical that you give people the choice in the matter: Whether they want to step and be the hero or not.

## Convention Five:

When I present the organization or programs to someone, they're going to want to see that every program has a track record of being in place for years, and it's done this and this already in the past before they can have confidence in it.

### Unconventional Approach Five:

A rather smart man, Albert Einstein, said that the definition of insanity is doing the same thing over and over again, and expecting different results. Failure after failure is all the conventional thinking has gotten us in solving these local, national, and global issues.

Certainly, you can wait several years and then jump on the bandwagon and if enough people have that same attitude, then no matter what's being done it's going to be too late to benefit millions.

Every successful business and program at one point didn't have a track record. From Apple Computer to Amazon to Ted Talks, the Peace Corps and UNICEF. They all started to address a perceived need, and regardless of the lack of a track record and growing pains, they were able to garner enough support to scale up and become major influencers in the world.

If the approach makes sense, and the program and systems are designed well, then the benefits far outweigh the fact that there is not yet a significant track record.

Based on the quality of the material and programs, you have to believe that the people behind them are going to do everything in their power to make them successful because the outcomes are so important.

To reinforce that point, that's why from the get-go, the programs are customizable and flexible so that they can be adopted to collaborate with so many institutions, so that they have the greatest likelihood of making an impact and being successful.

~~~

Our unconventional approach is designed to Outreach, Engage and Inspire people to take Action and work together for the Betterment of Kids, People and the Planet.

It's designed be disruptive and shake people free from the conventions that hold us down and prevent us from "Being The Hero". The time to Step Up and Act Is Now.

Think about it. What are the risks to ourselves, our families and our future if we don't enact the necessary global collaborative programs? Billions of people are fated to suffer from hardships for their entire remaining lives. You, me, everyone.

**We May Indeed Be Fighting for the Survival of The Human Race.**

# PREFACE

After spending many years developing the programs that would become the foundation for Planned Acts of Kindness, 2020 was the year we were to engage the world.

On February 24, 2020, I spoke at the United Nations about collaborating on a "16 Things We All Can Do To Act Right & Help Save The Planet" book on mental health issues and solutions for youth. They overwhelmingly agreed to do it.

In March 2020, I was scheduled to speak at the Excel conference of Wesleyan Churches (109 Churches from the Northeastern District) to promote our collaboration on publishing a 16 Things book on family issues such as substance abuse, domestic violence, finances, health, and education.

The Women's Prosperity Network (WPN) had agreed to do a 16 Things book on women's leadership for their global community.

Two weeks after I met with the United Nations it was shut down, the Excel conference in March never occurred. Neither did the women's prosperity book, nor the book that we were talking to Pfizer's Sustainability Department about doing to improve employee safety around the world, nor the book with Kroger Groceries on food, loss, hunger, and waste. Our popular summer internship/mentorship program which put 25 undergraduate and grad students in our office in New York for a three-month training program was also scrapped.

All died because of Covid. The virus was not only devastating to individuals and families, it was also devastating to organizations as well. The pandemic as a global issue was always built into the six tipping point issues that Planned Acts' Programs was created to address: Climate change, pollution, over population, pandemics, war, and terrorism.

But as far as I was concerned the tipping points made up only one aspect of our "Quality of Life" mission, the other issues we have to face and solve were also global social concerns: Financial inequality, health inequities and racial/religious/gender intolerance.

For the rest of 2020 and through 2021, I worked to develop additional books, programs, and initiatives to address the needs of our global family.

Just as Planned Acts of Kindness started as a program under my non-profit 16 Things Kids Can Do, One Planet One People was originally a mission that grew out of Planned Acts of Kindness.

Under the umbrella of One Planet One People, action areas developed and grew so quickly, so organically, that IPOP warranted its own status as a nonprofit organization in 2021.

Moving forward the question then became how to take our six action areas — books, courses, clubs, programs, events, and games — and present them to people in a way that doesn't overwhelm and gives them the opportunity to participate while achieving their own objectives.

And that's when I came up with the idea for the ONE book: One book that would bring everything together and show people how ONE person can make a difference in the world. And that ONE person is you.

**Be The Change You Want To See In The World. Be The Hero.**

## FOREWORD
### By Alice Mok

Early in my professional education at RMIT University in Melbourne Australia I gravitated toward the people aspects of architecture and interior design. I felt that architecture doesn't have to be mostly about the aesthetics, its very functionality should be of service to people. As the Lead Architect for many leading companies, I used my position to move even more into the realm of environmental sustainability and egalitarianism with my designs.

This is what makes my collaboration with Planned Acts of Kindness and One Planet One People so exciting for me personally. When I first met Lyle Benjamin and he learned what I did, he immediately envisioned a corporate architectural program that worked for the benefit of employees while at the same time fulfilling the business needs of companies where they worked.

The gist of the program Lyle created creating four separate working hubs starting with more traditional centralized space and then moving further afield into increasingly smaller hubs that shifted workspace benefits more to workers: i.e., reducing the time and expense of commutes, increasing the convenience and comfort of the working environment while still affording technological advantages.

But this wasn't where the greatest innovation came into play, it was Lyle's vision of the additional work/life balance programs he had created — kindness, volunteering, global citizenship, financial literacy, team building and much more — and how they could be integrated seamlessly with corporate and architectural constructs.

To be honest, I was a more than a little surprised at the depth of program he just created, and even more astounded when I began to think about the impact it could have on people all over the world.

But the question remained, could he deliver on what he spoke about? We have all experienced people that are good talkers, people that have a good idea, but what separates the 1 or 2 percent at the top is their ability to put into action their vision.

I was more than happy to learn that Lyle is one of these people. Not only did he develop the program, but he also wrote the copy, did art direction and designed the graphics which you see in The ONE Book. And he did this while suffering tremendously from 24/7 headaches due to long COVID.

During my career, I have been blessed to work with the leading companies of the world and get to know people at the highest levels of corporate big business. I'm telling you; I can't wait to share the **ONE** book and introduce them to Lyle. I know I'll be right there, up front, doing my part to make things happen.

P.S. If you have a green product or service, we want to learn more and see if you would qualify to be a Collaboration Partner in IPOP's One Green World EduMart. To get the process started, go to the PAK app and share!

# INTRODUCTION
## The Single Most Important Thing We Need To Do To Survive

Over the next ten years or so what do you think is going to be the most important issue facing humanity? Climate change? Pollution? Overpopulation? Pandemics? War? Terrorism? The fight against social injustices? Racism? Health Inequities? Economic and wealth inequality?

While these problems are all global quality of life issues, the single most important issue we face is combating fractionalism — approaching global issues that threaten the health and well-being of billions of people with a divided approach to education, resources, and solutions.

The only viable solution to pushing back on these tipping point issues is by employing collaborative systems that unite people on common causes with a common purpose from the grassroots up, and institutions from the top down.

In order to be scalable on the numbers and engage hundreds of millions of people, these collaborative programs and initiatives have to be diverse enough to resonate with people of different interests, ages, genders, races, nationalities, educations and incomes.

This is precisely the challenge that our combined non-profits take on in the **ONE** book. To collaborate with five groups of individuals and five types of institutional partners, Planned Acts of Kindness and One Planet One People have six main actionable areas that are fully scalable and customizable: Books/Workshops, Courses, Clubs, Activities, Events, and Games.

The point is you don't have to connect with everything we do. You don't have to agree with 90% of our initiatives and the delivery systems we use. You just have to find the ONE thing that resonates and excites you to take action and "Be The Hero."

This is your invitation to become part of the revolution that will change the world for billions. You can either join in or wait to see what develops. Our thoughts for those that choose to wait — we hope the issues don't come to your doorstep before you decide to get involved.

**The Time To Act Is Now**

**Lyle Benjamin, Founder**
Planned Acts of Kindness
One Planet One People

P.S. Page 115. I know there's a small group of people that can't resist flipping to the end of a book to find out how it turns out. For the ONE book, I'm enthusiastically encouraging everyone engage in this extremely inappropriate activity. Break the convention, take action and "Be The Hero" the world needs.

# SECTION 1:
# IT'S ABOUT YOU

"Strength does not come from physical capacity. It comes from an indomitable will."
— Mahatma Gandhi

# ABOUT YOU & THIS BOOK
## PLANNED ACTS OF KINDNESS (PAK) · ONE PLANET ONE PEOPLE (1POP)

### HOW TO GET THE MOST OUT OF THESE PAGES FOR YOURSELF, YOUR FAMILY & YOUR "COMMUNITY"

| 1. Get An Overview: | 2. What Grabs You? | 3. Scan The QR Code | 4. Use "NAV Menu" Explore & Volunteer |
|---|---|---|---|
| **Flip Through All The Pages In One Sitting** | **Circle Back To Those Programs** | **Get PAK App** | **Be The Hero & Share!** |

### TO SOLVE GLOBAL QUALITY OF LIFE ISSUES WE MUST COLLABORATE TO SUCCEED ... BE THE HERO!

WHERE | CAN | YOU | BRING | OUR | COLLAB. | PROGRAMS?

| HOMES | SCHOOLS | FAITH-BASED | NPOs/NGOs | COMPANIES | GOVERNMENTS |
|---|---|---|---|---|---|

### THE MAGNITUDE OF WHAT YOU CAN DO WHEN YOU'RE ENGAGED IN THE RIGHT SYSTEM ...

**RANDOM ACTS** | Vs. | **PLANNED ACTS OF KINDNESS** | & | **POWER OF ONE RIPPLE EFFECT**

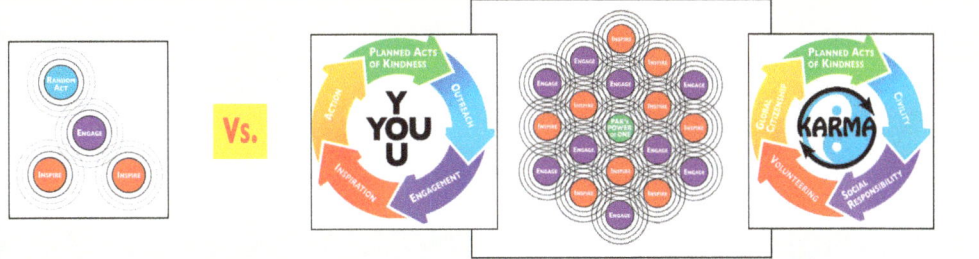

### OCCASIONALLY THOUGHT OF QUESTIONS ...

**Why are these pages here?**
*So you can see the Quality of Life programs offered by Planned Acts and One Planet One People.*

**Are you trying to sell me something?**
*No. We are a network of Non-Profit Organizations that work for the betterment of Kids, People and the Planet.*

**Why should I care? I already do enough.**
*Because your family, friends, neighbors, your community, your country and the planet needs your help, and one person can make a difference in the world.*

**I'm already pretty busy with work & family.**
*We understand and respect that. You always get to choose the time and scope of your involvement. Everything you do is welcome — from a simple planned act of kindness to sharing our org with someone you meet ... to bringing our programs into local schools or your workplace. It's all welcome, appreciated and needed.*

**It's a lot of pages, how do I manage that?**
*Explore as much or as little in a sitting as you're comfortable doing or do a Section at a time. It's all good!*

# MANY PATHS TO BE THE HERO
## PLANNED ACTS OF KINDNESS (PAK) • ONE PLANET ONE PEOPLE (1POP)

**PATH 1** YOUR DAILY PLANNED ACT OF KINDNESS IS TO SMILE MORE & PASS IT ON TO OTHERS. SIMPLE.

IT COSTS US NOTHING TO SMILE & WE ALL COULD USE A LITTLE MORE HAPPINESS IN OUR LIVES.

**PATH 2** YOU FEEL YOUTH NEED TO HAVE CIVILITY & KINDNESS TAUGHT IN SCHOOLS FROM FOUR YEARS UP.

AS A PARENT, SCHOOL ADMIN., TEACHER, STUDENT OR ALUM INTRODUCE 1POP'S E-QL PROGRAM TO YOUR PTO, ...

**PATH 3** YOU'RE EXCITED ABOUT THE 100 IN 100 DAYS COLLABORATION CAMPAIGN & YOU WANT TO INVITE

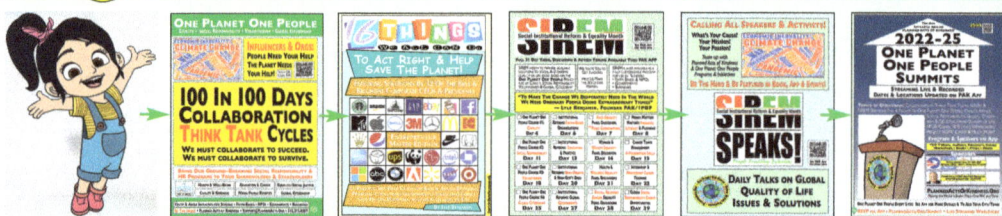

PEOPLE IN YOUR PROFESSION TO BE INTERVIEWED AS FEATURED EXPERTS FOR A 16 THINGS BOOK & WORKSHOP SERIES

**PATH 4** YOU WORK TO EARN MONEY FOR YOURSELF, YOUR FAMILY & YOUR FUTURE, BUT YOU'RE ALSO SMART

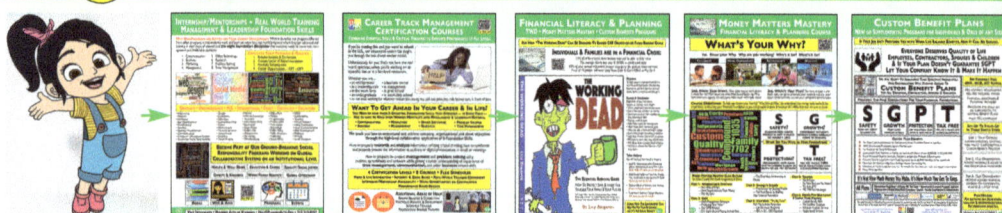

20 SMART ENOUGH TO KNOW THAT THERE'S MORE YOU CAN LEARN THAT CAN TAKE YOU TO THE NEXT LEVEL

## THE KARMA CLUB
### THE MORE YOU DO, THE GREATER YOUR REWARDS

PLANNED ACTS OF KINDNESS • "BE THE HERO" & JOIN US TODAY

## TO SOLVE THE PROBLEMS OF THE WORLD WE MUST COME TOGETHER AS ONE PLANET ONE PEOPLE

PLANNED ACTS OF KINDNESS INVITES YOU TO JOIN WITH PEOPLE ALL OVER THE WORLD IN TAKING

### THE GREAT PIZZA PEACE PLAN CHALLENGE

"I hereby make a PAK to treat others with respect and kindness and to go through life from this day forward acting towards others as I would wish to be treated myself. This is (name) from (city/country) for PlannedActs.Org"

2022-25 GOALS | 200+ COUNTRIES | 100's OF MILLIONS ENGAGED

"I think we're going to need to order more pizza!"

"No problem. Magic delivers!"

STEP UP. BE THE HERO! PROGRAMS FOR FAMILIES • FRIENDS • GROUPS • CLUBS • TEAMS • SCHOOLS • ORGS • BUSINESSES • GOVERNMENTS

## PROJECT KOPE
### HEALTH, HAPPINESS & WELLNESS THROUGH KINDNESS

ANXIOUS? STRESSED? LONELY? DEPRESSED?

We're Here to Help.

Youth & Adult Health & Wellness thru Kindness

Project KOPE

## THE ULTIMATE VOLUNTEERING CHALLENGE:
### JOIN CAAP: CRAZY AMBITIOUS ACTIVITIES PROGRAM

LIVE YOUR PASSION! SPORTS • CELEBRITY • SCHOOL • FAITH • GOV'T

## CREATING LEGACIES FOR LOST LOVED ONES
MEMORIAL BOOKS CAN BE BRANDED FOR ORGANIZATIONS AS GIVE-AWAYS

### HELP HEAL COVID-19 FAMILIES

## LEGACY LIFELINES
# Memorial

Keeping the Joy & Happiness Alive for You, Your Family & Generations to Come

By Lyle Benjamin
Founder of Non-Profit Planned Acts of Kindness

## ONE PLANET ONE PEOPLE PORTAL
CONNECTING PEOPLE TO COLLABORATIVE GLOBAL SYSTEMS
BASED ON KINDNESS TO ENSURE E-QUALITY OF LIFE FOR ALL

The World Is In Crisis: From Climate Change To Pandemics Do You Have What It Takes To Join Others Around The World & Be The Hero?

All Nationalities All Languages All Ages All Welcome!

Share Here! World Video Map

Your Quest Starts Here! Enter The Portal

AMBASSADORS & INFLUENCERS WANTED!
YOUR COUNTRY NEEDS YOU & THE WORLD NEEDS YOU

• CIVILITY & KINDNESS
• HEALTH & WELL-BEING
• EQUALITY/SOCIAL JUSTICE
• EDUCATION & CAREER TRAINING
• WORK & FAMILY BENEFITS
• GLOBAL CITIZENSHIP

HELP BRING OUR GLOBAL SOCIAL RESPONSIBILITY "ENGAGEMENT & ACTION" PROGRAMS INTO SCHOOLS, FAITH-BASED ORGS, NPOs/NGOs, BUSINESSES & GOVERNMENTS

## STEP UP & INSPIRE OTHERS TO "BE THE HERO" FOR OUR FAMILIES, FRIENDS & FUTURE: QUALITY OF LIFE FOR ALL

COMING SOON "THE ALLIANCE"

# SECTION II:
# OKAY, A LITTLE BIT ABOUT US

> "AS WE EXPRESS OUR
> GRATITUDE, WE MUST
> NEVER FORGET
> THAT THE HIGHEST
> APPRECIATION IS NOT
> TO UTTER WORDS,
> BUT TO LIVE BY THEM."
> — JOHN F. KENNEDY

# THE STORY & POWER OF PLANNED ACTS

Through the website, its apps, and "Host & Post" partner program, Planned Acts of Kindness automatically provides the "What you can do" on a daily basis to help others.

Every day, what you can do is right there in front of you. All you have to do is take action. And the more you do, the more you'll want to do because of how it helps others and helps yourself at the same time.

Members of the Karma Club are automatically provided with the "How" to document, record and track their actions, and receive rewards based on karma and achievements.

As for the "Why" of it? Well, in addition to the Karma Club rewards, there are many compelling reasons "Why" we need to change to a more proactive lifestyle based on kindness.

Why Do Your Planned Acts? One reason is that helping others is just the right thing for us to do as a species. For too long, we have been divided by a growing lack of civility toward others that don't share our views or behaviors. We have the power of choice, and it's time we actively worked at helping people in need regardless of nationality, religion, gender, age, education, or income.

There is an ever increasing lack of civility in our country and the world: Where if you don't think like me, you must automatically be my enemy. And this lack of civility is literally destroying lives.

It was this same adversarial mentality and approach to every situation that led me to quit the legal professional. I felt that there were more productive (healthier and less costly) approaches to resolving conflict.

Also, in my capacity as the Executive Director of an NPO that works with other organizations and churches, I got to see the results of people doing volunteer work, or what I call random acts of kindness. And oftentimes their efforts, although appreciated, weren't really that impactful on a long-term basis.

I created Planned Acts of Kindness to give people fun, easy, consistent and sustainable programs, initiatives and systems to help other people in their community, country and in the world, while directly benefiting themselves through the effects of positive, powerful actions and a gamified rewards program — where The More You Do, the Greater Your Rewards."

Most of us have heard stories on the news about someone who has done some random act of kindness that really tugged at our collective heartstrings. For the vast majority of us sitting at home or at work on our sofas and chairs, the feelings registered and were gone with the introduction of the next commercial. And that's the rub. Most of us would like to do more to help others, but until now we didn't have a system to make it doable, and lacking the means, we remained firmly entrenched on our backsides. (No offense intended. I have a backside too.)

Another reason is that helping others on a sustained basis grants you, the do-gooder, with more than Karmic rewards: People with active social connections to family, friends, and community are happier, healthier — physically and mentally. Studies show they live longer than people who are less well connected. So, the more you do, the greater are your rewards in these essential Quality of Life areas.

# OUR MISSION & VISION
## PLANNED ACTS OF KINDNESS (PAK) • ONE PLANET ONE PEOPLE (1POP)

**LYLE BENJAMIN, FOUNDER**

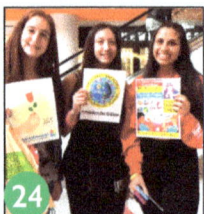

**PAK:** Planned Acts of Kindness was conceived in November of 2016 with the objective of providing Quality of Life for All through a more unified world by instilling a greater sense of civility, ethics, social responsibility, volunteerism and global citizenship in people. In 2021, Benjamin launched **ONE PLANET ONE PEOPLE** first as an environment platform, and then as an umbrella movement to unite people and institutions around the globe on tipping point and quality of life issues that require immediate global action. In the short time since their launch, dozens of schools, NPOs, NGOs, government agencies and businesses have expressed their support for Planned Acts' programs.

**QUALITY OF LIFE MISSION:** Planned Acts of Kindness is a 501(c)3 non-profit global outreach platform where people wake up and on their cell phone, computer or device there is a new daily "Planned Act of Kindness" that they can do with their family, friends, coworkers and in their community. The goal is to have tens of millions of people around the country, hundreds of millions of people around the world, waking up and doing the same thing on the same day, and unleashing that much powerful, positive energy in the world.

**PLANNED ACTS & KARMA:** The key to living happier, healthier lives is not how much money you make or how much "drugs" you take, but rather the quality of your relationships and your sense of community. Planned Acts enhances these two things for people. And to better keep people engaged we gamified it. There are different four achievements that people can do during the month: Daily PAKs, Engagement, Volunteering and Support. And when you do these four activities during the month, you can level up, and then you're eligible for free gifts that we give away every single day to random people at that level. So, it's like Karma, "The More You Do, The Greater Your Rewards."

**THE TIPPING POINTS:** Now, the problems of the world — climate change, pollution, overpopulation pandemics, war and terrorism — these problems are not going to be solved governments or corporations alone. They're going to be solved by ordinary people around the world working together on common causes with a common focus, and that's what the Karma Club can also help do.

We can have millions of people in the Karma Club taking individual responsibility on these problems, and they can come to together get governments and corporations to change their behavior. We have one planet and one people on the planet. The tipping points aren't 20 years or 30 years from now. They are now. And if we don't start acting like it, then life on this planet will be tremendously different for billons of people, and not in a positive way.

**CSR HERO'S WANTED:** To outreach, engage and inspire to reach our goals, we need your financial help to produce our books, courses, summits, workshops, games and products. Our Sponsorship and Corporate Social Responsibility programs have various levels of support designed to reach upwards of hundreds of millions at the highest level.

This is a unique opportunity to outreach and engage millions in positive Social Responsibility activities over a sustained period using multiple programs that inspire, recognize and reward people for their actions. Due to these connections, we have numerous organizational requests for our books, courses, summits, and workshops, and require funding for additional staff and production. Help us produce the programs we need to make 2022: The Year of "One Planet One People."

**PAK** **PLANNEDACTS.ORG**
MAKING THE WORLD A BETTER PLACE, ONE PAK AT A TIME!

# THE FOUNDER'S WHY

I didn't start out wanting to change the world, I just wanted to repay a debt. I was born three months premature and weighed two pounds three ounces and I spent the first four and half months of my life in an incubator.

When I was seven my parents divorced which even to me seemed like a good plan. Afterwards, I taught myself how to cook. In part to help my mom out because she seemed overwhelmed. In part because she was such a bad cook that she would burn frozen fish sticks.

At 11 years old I felt there was too much discord in the house between my siblings. So, I brought it up with my mother and asked if she were going to do anything about it. She told me she was doing the best she could.

I felt I had my answer. The same day I went to school and told everyone I was leaving — it would be my last day. In the evening I called my father and told him I would like to live with him. For him it was a moral victory that one of his six children chose him over my mother. For me, I was sensitive and just wanted to get away from the conflicts. Little did I know that I was leaving the proverbial frying pan and going into the fire.

My father was authoritarian, controlling and at best verbally insensitive. At worse verbally and emotionally abusive. Mostly to get out of the house to escape criticism, I ventured out into the streets of New York City looking for work. I got hired to do deliveries for a neighborhood florist and ended up having a talent for floral decoration and customer service. I also met store owners and managers that I remember to this day.

Jim was the 6' 3" bear bellied (I don't know if he drank beer) manager of the fast-food fried chicken place down the block. He would stop by and say let's have lunch, and he'd treat me to food while we sat on wooden crates in the back talking about life. I remember wondering, "I'm an eleven-year-old know-nothing kid, why is he taking the time out of his busy day to befriend me?" Not only did he treat me with kindness Jim spoke to me like I was an adult friend that he liked and respected. It was definitely not the treatment I had ever received at home.

Growing up I felt that sometimes people were not always kind or good. At a young age, I decided I wanted to be a veterinarian because animals couldn't communicate when they had difficulties, so I could be their advocate.

At 13, my father relocated us to Florida to be closer to his engineering and building projects. When I was 14, I went around to some veterinarian businesses and asked if I could volunteer. Despite having a constant barrage of college students apply, the owner of Dania Sterling Animal Clinic accepted my offer and took me under his wing.

During my time there we talked about a lot of personal things in addition to work. I learned how to assist with everything from removing tartar on dog teeth with a drill to unplugging hair blockages in cats (don't ask), to spading and castration.

But Dr. Scott showed me much more than this, he showed me what it was to be a really kind and generous person. He helped me deal with an abusive home situation when he didn't have to. He gave me money when he didn't have to. He treated me with respect, kindness, and friendship when he didn't have to.

From Jim to Dr. Scott to numerous others including parents of friends, people I met through work, teachers, and administrators at schools, I realized that these people saved me. Instead of withdrawing or acting out, I got support that helped me cope on a day-to-day basis even when our time together had ended.

I knew I couldn't repay their kindness directly and show them the gratitude that I felt, so I decided that I would work to help others through my career. That's when I made the switch to my second career choice: I would become a lawyer and help people.

The only problem was I sucked at school. I didn't learn how to read until I was in third grade and put in a special remedial reading class with individual

# KINDNESS & GRATITUDE

attention. I was also given speech lessons because of my pronunciation. When I moved to my dad's, I ended up going to an experimental school for seventh and eighth grade. I studied Greek mythology for a year. Didn't have math or science classes because they couldn't find instructors. And read a couple of hundred books for entertainment.

When we moved to Florida and I started high school, I was undisciplined and lacked the fundamental knowledge that others had received in middle school. Not a good combination for success. But it turned out that my teachers and classmates felt I had some brains and a good personality, and that was a good enough combination.

In the middle of my junior year, we moved again, and my new school administered an IQ test before placing me in classes. I was a C+ student but tested well enough for them to place me in the Talented and Gifted (TAGS) Program. It was there that I discovered literary analysis, and my interest in writing and design.

In my senior year, I won first place in district in a magazine layout competition despite never formally studying it. My father was sitting at the kitchen table when I came home and showed him the trophy. He looked up from what he was reading and said, "You really like doing that stuff?" "Yes," I replied, and he went back to his papers without another word.

I was also involved in sports: Gymnastics and tennis in school and fencing and table tennis on my own. For the first time I was fully enjoying school and doing well. I was friends with students in all the clicks, I was close with teachers and even administrators in a school with over 2,000 students.

It was during this time that my father and stepmother decided I should graduate high school six months early so I could earn money for college. Like with many things in my home life, I didn't agree but went along with it regardless.

We lived in rural Fort Lauderdale and the nearest town was nine miles away. Coincidentally my school was also nine miles away. So, the day after I graduated early, I took the school bus and told teachers, administrators, and friends that I was looking for a job and then walked into town and knocked on some businesses.

After taking the bus back home that afternoon, my stepmother accused me of going to school to just socialize and not being interested in finding a job. When I told her that unless she was willing to drive me in, when she wasn't, then I would continue to take the school bus because I wasn't going to walk to town.

She didn't take too kindly to this and started cursing me out and knocking my books to the floor.

When I escorted her from my room, she told my father that she wanted "your @#$%@#$ son out of the @#$%@#$ house." When I spoke with him, he seemed to agree, having already told me in the past that even though I might be right about my objections or differences, he would always side with her because it made his life easier.

I had my answer. When a friend of mine, Steve, came over later that evening to pick me up to go to a school event, I explained the situation. He immediately volunteered that I could come live with him and his parents. I left that night.

Two days after graduating early at 17 years old and one month I got a job with the largest bookstore in South Florida through a friend at school. Over the next nine months I worked my way up from stocking shelves to be the floor manager in charge of magazines and then new book purchases. I worked an average of 63 hours a week and saved around three thousand dollars. I happily did chores around Steve's house to repay their generosity.

Unfortunately, I was still a minor and dependent on my father's signature on my papers to attend college. He refused to sign. I arranged to get a court appointed social worker who was supposed to look after my interests. But after our first meeting I felt he was siding with my father. I knew I needed help, and since I was already at the Miami courthouse, I decided to see if a judge would do it. I walked into the first judge's office I found and said to the woman behind the desk, "I have a problem, and I was wondering if the judge could help me."

As I started to explain, she called over another woman and they sat down and listened as I described the situation. When I was done, they both agreed they would help. And help they did. They ended up drafting the documents I needed to sue my father for non-support. Boy, was he surprised when he got served with papers to appear in court.

My father was a proud man. Getting sued by his 17-year-old son who he always thought of as emotional and weak, fundamentally changed his view of me. He now admired the "guts" it took for me to sue him. to do it. For myself, it was not about forcing him to support me or give me money. I simply wanted to go to school, and my only recourse to stand up to a bully was to get a bigger, stronger bully on my side.

I agreed to meet with him at my old house where I learned my stepmother, Yvette, was pregnant. During the meeting my father was acting civil, friendly even. He said he would sign my college papers and asked if I would drop the suit. Partially because he was being nice and partially because my stepmother was pregnant, I agreed right away.

The start of my fresh-man year at the University of Florida was still months away, and I was invited back to my high school to attend the end of the year formal graduation of seniors. During the awards announcements, I was surprised to hear my name called and I was ushered on stage. In front a packed auditorium I learned I had been awarded the Morris Cooper scholarship and given $500 to be used for purchasing textbooks in college.

I was completely humbled again. For the administrators to show that much generosity to a student that was only at the school for the last half his junior year and first half of his senior year really touched me.

But this wasn't all. For months following the time I was kicked out of the house, Mrs. Hughes, my ex-humanities teacher had asked me to keep a journal. I wrote down the things I was going through, the things I thought, my feelings and experiences and once a week we would meet and talk. I gave her my writings and she turned them over to the typing teacher Mrs. Bowling. Every week I would get back a stack of pages we would discuss.

Neither one of them had to do this. It went over and above anything they had to do for students let alone ex-students. And I appreciated every conversation and every page I received. Whether they knew it or not, they all served to reinforce my desire to help others so I could repay the kindness they had so willingly given.

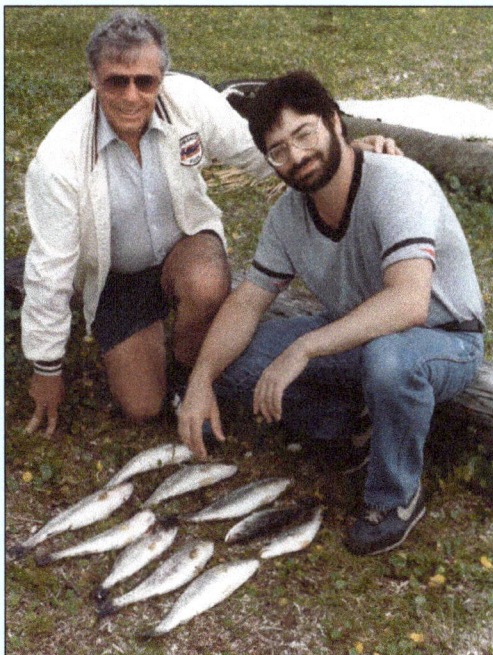

I did go to law school and then worked as an intern in the Litigation Bureau in the Attorney General's Office in Albany, New York writing memorandums of law on public health and other issues. What I learned was that I didn't like the way the professors taught, didn't like the reasons my friends wanted to become attorneys, didn't like the fact that there was very little practical application in what was taught, and didn't like the main methodology used for conflict resolution. I knew there were better, less costly ways to resolve conflict and decided the profession wasn't suited for my goals of helping people, so I took a permanent leave of absence.

While an undergraduate I had a sideline business of resume writing and paper editing which I kept alive while I was in law school. After I left law school, I expanded it into a marketing, design, and printing business. I felt that I could further develop my skills in these areas, and it would help me throughout my lifetime achieve my goals.

# FINDING GOODNESS IN GOD

My time with my father had never been better. He now treated me with respect and affection, and we were able to share many things about our lives including our affinity for business. He even hired me to set up a dedicated computer system to handle his customized engineering proposals. Still, I hadn't realized how much he came to appreciate the change in our dynamics until one visit he surprised me with an offer of 50% equity in his engineering company.

I told him I was flattered especially since I didn't know anything about engineering. "I know how your mind works," he told me. "The engineering I can teach you. You'll have no problem handling the technical aspects. But what I can't find after all my years in business is someone who has the combination of technical, and high-level business and communication skills that you have."

Even though I didn't take him up on his offer, we continued enjoying the relationship. On a subsequent visit to south Florida, I happened to be looking over the book titles in his wall unit. He came up and pulled a book off one of the shelves. "Read this," he said putting the book in my hand. "You'll enjoy it." It was the autobiography of the life of test pilot Chuck Yeager, and it was the first time he had ever given me a book to read in my life.

A few weeks later I had finished the book and I decided to call him to talk about it. It was the middle of the workday, and we both had companies to run. We talked for quite a while and one of the take-aways we both had about the book was that Yeager had given up test flying because he had the feeling that his days were numbered. If he kept it up it would kill him.

That was the last time we spoke. The following week I got a call from a family friend saying that my father, stepmother, and little sister Melissa were killed in a plane crash the night before. I had given my stepmother the idea for the name Melissa while on a call with her from college. Melissa was only nine years old.

Since he was a kid, my father had always loved aviation. He had been a pilot for decades and was licensed to fly everything from private planes to commercial jets. He was always meticulously careful when it came to safety.

While flying over the Chesapeake Bay the night before a sudden storm developed from the remnants of a passing hurricane hundreds of miles away. The plane was struck by lightning, and he lost instrumentation including the altimeter which pilots their distance above land.

He alerted the nearest airport control tower of his emergency and while coming in for the landing they diverted him to a different approach. When he banked the plane to turn to the new heading, the wing tip of the twin engine Cessna hit the water. The plane disintegrated on impact.

I was devastated. My friend Jon came over to my business to check on me and ended up driving me aimlessly around town in his truck. To honor my father, we went to a deli, and I ate a pastrami on rye while crying the entire time. It took me months to recover. For only the second time in my life, I experienced depression.

Hurricanes were developing more frequently and becoming more dangerous. It was the harbinger of what was to come. I realize later that subconsciously it developed into the motivation for my on-going battle to stop climate change from devastating people's lives, just as it had mine.

During this heartbreaking and emotionally devastating time surrounding the death of my father, I managed to piece together details of events that I experienced: From the Chuck Yaeger book to my last phone call, and many others, I took solace from the fact that God was looking out for me. God gave me these comforting events, I just had to be open enough and willing enough to understand their significance.

Six months later I followed my father's other wish for me, I sold my printing company and moved to New York City. I knew no one, but I had a vision of what I wanted to do to help fulfill my mission. I had created a prototype for a ground-breaking magazine on helping people deal with the complexities inherent in all types of relationships: Intimate, family, friendship, and work.

I pitched it to just two companies: Time Warner and Kable News. Both offered me contracts, and six months later my magazine, "Relationships Today" was on newsstands across the country.

At last I was on my journey to pay back other people's kindness.

# EXECUTIVE SUMMARY
## PLANNED ACTS OF KINDNESS (PAK) • ONE PLANET ONE PEOPLE (1POP)

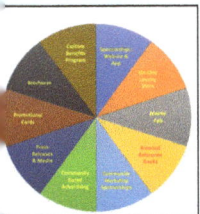

**QUALITY OF LIFE MISSION:** What makes Planned Acts so inspirational for individuals and other organizations is the inspiration of our Quality of Life mission, the breadth and depth of our programs, and the viability of our systems.

**SPONSORED ENGAGEMENT, EDUCATION & ACTION PROGRAMS:**
**GLOBAL CITIZENSHIP:** Planned Acts of Kindness Global Social Responsibility Platform
   The Karma Club: Gamification of Social Responsibility Actions providing recognition/rewards
**BOOK SERIES:** "16 Things We All Can Do To Act Right & Help Save The Planet" Special Edition
   • 100,000 Co-Branded Books reaching 500,000 readers  • CEO featured on cover/forward
   • Chapter on your Mission  • 8 full pages in 4C  • Up to 55,000 free books for promo use
**BOOK-BASED WORKSHOPS:** Over 20,000+ attendees for 8-12 week peer-to-peer workshops
**ONE PLANET ONE PEOPLE CLUBS:** Engaging Schools & Communities with Lifelong Support
**COURSES/CLASSES:** Education/Action Courses in 1POP 4 Pillars; Career Track Management
8-Foundation Skill Certification; Money Matters Mastery Financial Literacy & Planning Course
   • Use in Businesses, Schools, Faith-Based & Non-Profit Orgs, Govt. Agencies
**CORPORATE SOCIAL RESPONSIBILITY PROGRAMS (CSR):**
   • Branded App tracking, recognition and rewards on company engagement objectives for
Shareholders, Stakeholders on custom topics such as Education, Sustainability, Health/Safety
   • "Be The Hero" Leadership, Recognition & Rewards CSR Program
   • (No Fee) Financial Literacy & Planning Custom Benefit Programs for workers and families
**SUMMITS/EVENTS:** 2022: The Year of One Planet One People: Live streaming Summits in
United States & other Countries to Outreach, Engage, Inspire & Educate People to Action

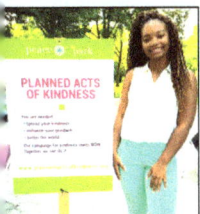

**ENDORSEMENTS:**
*"What you're doing is great. I'm glad you're taking on this project. We definitely need it. We've become so, let's just call, divided in our country and when we are just talking being human beings, about solving problems we all share, it doesn't matter what side of the political spectrum you're on."*
**— Jack Canfield,** *Best-Selling Author of "Chicken Soup for the Soul" and "The Success Principles"*

*"This is such a wonderful program, and such an important program. It's absolutely needed, and I encourage everyone to get involved!"*
**— Trish Carr,** *Business Success Coach and Co-Founder of the Women's Prosperity Network*

*"I really see how this program can be a game changer. It's tremendously ambitious, but it has what it takes to make it happen."*
**— Steve Harrison,** *Bradley Communications. Founder of National Publicity Summit, Network & Radio/TV Interview Report (helped successfully launch "Rich Dad, Poor Dad" "Chicken Soup for the Soul" "Men Are From Mars ..."*

**THE TIME TO GET INVOLVED IS NOW:** We invite you to join our extraordinary system of programs that unite communities around the country and around the globe under the umbrella of One Planet One People. When you join us, your organization will be recognized as one of the leaders in Corporate Social Responsibility; part of the team working on solutions to global issues and a major source of positive action and goodwill working for the betterment of kids, people and the planet.

JACK CANFIELD

PLANNED ACTS OF KINDNESS
& ACME, INC.
MAKING THE WORLD A BETTER PLACE,
ONE PAK AT A TIME
REGENT SPONSOR

**CONTACT FOUNDER LYLE BENJAMIN AT 212 213-0257 TO SEE HOW
OUR PROGRAMS CAN HELP YOU EXCEED YOUR OBJECTIVES**

29

# BOARD OF ADVISORS

**Jack Canfield**
Success Principles.
Santa Barbara CA

**Trish Carr** – Business &
Entrepreneurship.
Ft. Lauderdale FL

**Coumba Marenah**
UN & Global Leadership.
Wilmington MD

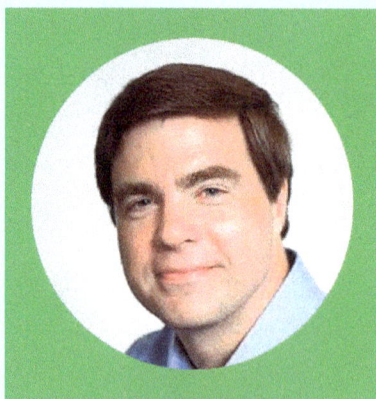

**Steve Harrison**
Publicity & Business Dev.
Philadelphia PA

**Rick Frishman**
Publishing, Guerilla Marketing.
New York NY

**Linda Hollander**
Corporate Sponsorship.
Los Angeles CA

"ALONE WE CAN
DO SO LITTLE;
TOGETHER WE CAN
DO SO MUCH."
— Helen Keller

# U.N. SUSTAINABLE DEVELOPMENT GOALS FOR 2030

SUSTAINABLE DEVELOPMENT GOALS

1 NO POVERTY
2 ZERO HUNGER
3 GOOD HEALTH AND WELL-BEING
4 QUALITY EDUCATION
5 GENDER EQUALITY
6 CLEAN WATER AND SANITATION
7 AFFORDABLE AND CLEAN ENERGY
8 DECENT WORK AND ECONOMIC GROWTH
9 INDUSTRY, INNOVATION AND INFRASTRUCTURE
10 REDUCED INEQUALITIES
11 SUSTAINABLE CITIES AND COMMUNITIES
12 RESPONSIBLE CONSUMPTION AND PRODUCTION
13 CLIMATE ACTION
14 LIFE BELOW WATER
15 LIFE ON LAND
16 PEACE, JUSTICE AND STRONG INSTITUTIONS
17 PARTNERSHIPS FOR THE GOALS

## QUALITY OF LIFE FOR ALL MISSION:

To fullfil their Global missions, Planned Acts of Kindness and One Planet One People have outreach, engagement, education and action programs for all 17 of the United Nations Sustainable Development Goals.

| SDG | SUSTAINABLE DEVELOPMENT GOALS | U.N. | PAK | PROGRAMS | BOOKS | COURSES | SR CLUBS | EVENTS | GAMES | CSR |
|---|---|---|---|---|---|---|---|---|---|---|
| 1. | No Poverty | ✔ | ✔ | ✔ | ✔ | ✔ | ✔ | ✔ | ✔ | — |
| 2. | Zero Hunger | ✔ | ✔ | ✔ | ✔ | ✔ | ✔ | ✔ | ✔ | |
| 3. | Good Health & Well-Being | ✔ | ✔ | ✔ | ✔ | ✔ | ✔ | ✔ | ✔ | ✔ |
| 4. | Quality Education | ✔ | ✔ | ✔ | ✔ | ✔ | ✔ | ✔ | ✔ | |
| 5. | Gender Equality | ✔ | ✔ | ✔ | | — | ✔ | — | — | ✔ |
| 6. | Water & Sanitation | ✔ | ✔ | ✔ | ✔ | ✔ | ✔ | ✔ | ✔ | ✔ |
| 7. | Affordable & Clean Energy | ✔ | ✔ | ✔ | ✔ | ✔ | ✔ | ✔ | ✔ | ✔ |
| 8. | Decent Work & Economic Growth | ✔ | ✔ | ✔ | ✔ | ✔ | ✔ | ✔ | ✔ | ✔ |
| 9. | Industry, Innovation & Infrastructure | ✔ | ✔ | ✔ | ✔ | — | ✔ | ✔ | ✔ | ✔ |
| 10. | Reduced Inequalities | ✔ | ✔ | ✔ | ✔ | ✔ | ✔ | ✔ | ✔ | ✔ |
| 11. | Sustainable Cities & Communities | ✔ | ✔ | ✔ | ✔ | ✔ | ✔ | ✔ | ✔ | ✔ |
| 12. | Responsible Consumption & Production | ✔ | ✔ | ✔ | ✔ | ✔ | ✔ | ✔ | ✔ | ✔ |
| 13. | Climate Action | ✔ | ✔ | ✔ | ✔ | ✔ | ✔ | ✔ | ✔ | ✔ |
| 14. | Life Below Water | ✔ | ✔ | ✔ | ✔ | ✔ | ✔ | ✔ | ✔ | ✔ |
| 15. | Life on Land | ✔ | ✔ | ✔ | ✔ | ✔ | ✔ | ✔ | ✔ | ✔ |
| 16. | Peace, Justice & Strong Institutions | ✔ | ✔ | ✔ | ✔ | ✔ | ✔ | ✔ | ✔ | ✔ |
| 17. | Partnerships for the Goals | ✔ | ✔ | ✔ | ✔ | ✔ | ✔ | ✔ | ✔ | ✔ |

# WHAT'S YOUR MISSION?
## DO YOU HAVE A CAUSE YOU WANT TO SUPPORT?

PLANNED ACTS & IPOP PROGRAMS ARE BASED ON COLLABORATION BETWEEN PEOPLE, INSTITUTIONS & COUNTRIES AND ARE BUILT ON THE PRINCIPLES OF:

CIVILITY
EQUALITY
EDUCATION

ONE PLANET ONE PEOPLE · GLOBAL ACTION PROGRAMS · PLANNEDACTS.ORG ·

CONTACT US

ACTION
INCLUSION
SUSTAINABILITY

## QUALITY OF LIFE FOR ALL

## FULLY CUSTOMIZABLE & SCALABLE PROGRAMS, BOOKS, COURSES, WORKSHOPS, ACTIVITIES, EVENTS

33

# WE ARE AT THE TIPPING POINT FOR HUMANITY. THIS DECADE WILL DETERMINE THE QUALITY OF LIFE FOR BILLIONS OF PEOPLE.

CLIMATE CHANGE

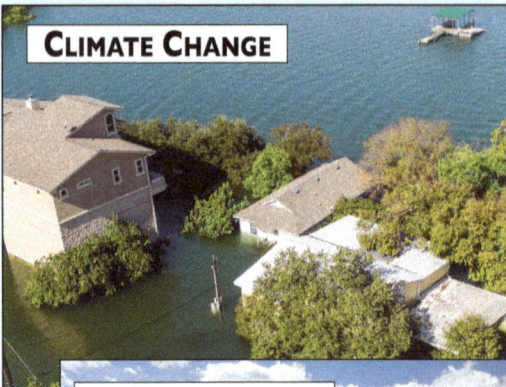

AND LIKE IT OR NOT, WE ARE ALL IN THIS TOGETHER.

**THE TIME FOR DIVISION IS OVER.**

POLLUTION

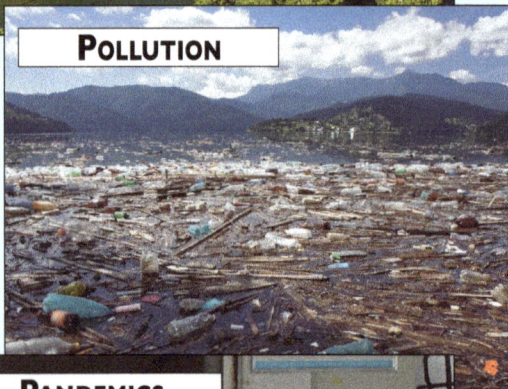

THE FRACTIONAL APPROACH TO SOLVING GLOBAL SOCIAL ISSUES DOESN'T WORK.

PANDEMICS

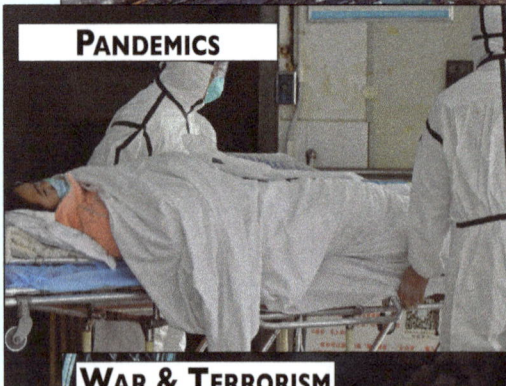

**WE MUST COLLABORATE TO SUCCEED.**

**WE MUST COLLABORATE TO SURVIVE.**

WAR & TERRORISM

SO, WHAT'S YOUR CAUSE? **WHAT'S YOUR PASSION?**

PAK WEB APP

WHAT CAN PAK & ONE PLANET ONE PEOPLE DO FOR YOU?

34

# ONE PLANET ONE PEOPLE

## CIVILITY • SOCIAL RESPONSIBILITY • VOLUNTEERISM • GLOBAL CITIZENSHIP

## INFLUENCERS & ORGS:
### PEOPLE NEED YOUR HELP, THE PLANET NEEDS YOUR HELP!

SCAN QR CODE FMI

# JOIN THE COLLABORATION THINK TANK NETWORK /CTTN

**100 IN 100 DAYS COLLABORATION THINK TANK CYCLES:**
100 INFLUENCERS, 100 BUSINESS LEADERS, 100 GOVT OFFICIALS, 100 NPO/NGO FOUNDERS, 100 EDUCATORS, 100 FAITH-BASED LEADERS

## WE MUST COLLABORATE TO SUCCEED.
## WE MUST COLLABORATE TO SURVIVE.

### BE THE HERO! WHO CAN YOU RECOMMEND?

## BRING OUR GROUND-BREAKING SOCIAL RESPONSIBILITY & HR PROGRAMS TO YOUR SHAREHOLDERS & STAKEHOLDERS

SUSTAINABLE DEVELOPMENT GOALS
IPOP / 17 UN SDGs

| HEALTH & WELL-BEING | EDUCATION & CAREER | EQUALITY/SOCIAL JUSTICE |
| --- | --- | --- |
| CIVILITY & KINDNESS | WORK/FAMILY BENEFITS | GLOBAL CITIZENSHIP |

YOUTH & ADULT INITIATIVES FOR: SCHOOLS • FAITH-BASED • NPOS/NGOS • GOVERNMENTS • BUSINESSES

BE THE HERO! • PLANNED ACTS OF KINDNESS • SUPPORT@PLANNEDACTS.ORG • 212.213.0257 (35)

# INFLU/ORGS: COLLABORATION THINK TANK NETWORK

## INDIVIDUAL & ORGANIZATIONAL SOCIAL RESPONSIBLITY FOR THE BETTERMENT OF KIDS, PEOPLE & THE PLANET

**1 — TAKE COLLABORATION PLEDGE, WORK GLOBALLY WITH OTHER INSTITUTIONS**

We are at the tipping point for humanity. This decade will determine the Quality-of-Life for billions of people on the planet. The time for division is over. The fractional approach to solving global issues doesn't work. We must collaborate to succeed. We must collaborate to survive. I hereby agree to join "The 100 in 100 Days Collaboration Campaign" and work with One Planet One People and Collaborative Partners to provide Quality-of-Life …

COMPLETE ON APP

**2 — TEAMS: CHOOSE FROM THE U.N. SDG COLLABORATION AREAS**

- INFLUENCERS **&**
- CORPORATIONS
- GOVT AGENCIES
- NPOs / NGOs
- FAITH-BASED ORGS
- EDUCATIONAL INST.

SUSTAINABLE DEVELOPMENT GOALS

1 NO POVERTY
2 ZERO HUNGER
3 GOOD HEALTH AND WELL-BEING
4 QUALITY EDUCATION
5 GENDER EQUALITY
6 CLEAN WATER AND SANITATION
7 AFFORDABLE AND CLEAN ENERGY
8 DECENT WORK AND ECONOMIC GROWTH
9 INDUSTRY, INNOVATION AND INFRASTRUCTURE
10 REDUCED INEQUALITIES
11 SUSTAINABLE CITIES AND COMMUNITIES
12 RESPONSIBLE CONSUMPTION AND PRODUCTION
13 CLIMATE ACTION
14 LIFE BELOW WATER
15 LIFE ON LAND
16 PEACE, JUSTICE AND STRONG INSTITUTIONS
17 PARTNERSHIPS FOR THE GOALS

**3 — SYSTEM: IPOP/PAK COLLABORATORS & ACTIONABLE PATHWAYS**

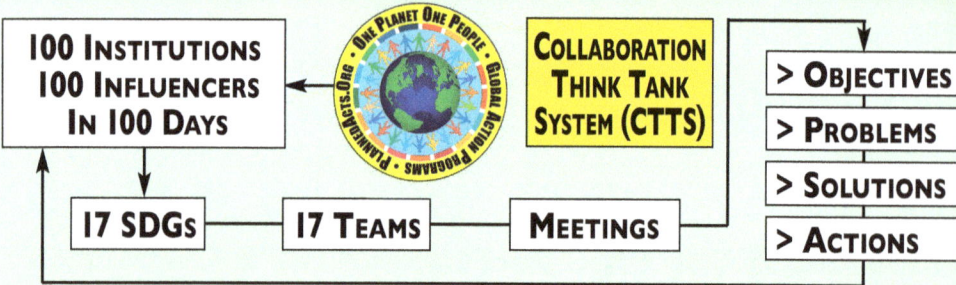

100 INSTITUTIONS
100 INFLUENCERS
IN 100 DAYS

ONE PLANET ONE PEOPLE · GLOBAL ACTION PROGRAMS · PLANETARYACTS.ORG ·

COLLABORATION THINK TANK SYSTEM (CTTS)

> OBJECTIVES
> PROBLEMS
> SOLUTIONS
> ACTIONS

17 SDGs — 17 TEAMS — MEETINGS

**4 — NETWORK: ENGAGE, EDUCATE & INSPIRE PEOPLE TO TAKE ACTION ON ISSUES**

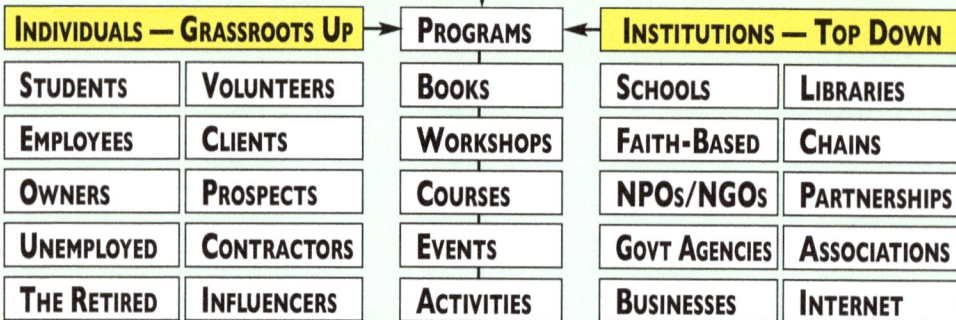

| INDIVIDUALS — GRASSROOTS UP | | PROGRAMS | INSTITUTIONS — TOP DOWN | |
|---|---|---|---|---|
| STUDENTS | VOLUNTEERS | BOOKS | SCHOOLS | LIBRARIES |
| EMPLOYEES | CLIENTS | WORKSHOPS | FAITH-BASED | CHAINS |
| OWNERS | PROSPECTS | COURSES | NPOs/NGOs | PARTNERSHIPS |
| UNEMPLOYED | CONTRACTORS | EVENTS | GOVT AGENCIES | ASSOCIATIONS |
| THE RETIRED | INFLUENCERS | ACTIVITIES | BUSINESSES | INTERNET |

**2022-25 QUARTERLY COLLABORATION CYCLES: ADD 500+ INSTITUTIONS & INFLUENCERS/2,000 ANNUALLY**

**PAK**

**ONE PLANET ONE PEOPLE**

**0** | U.S. LEADING THE WORLD IN PRISON POPULATION, EXPENSE, PHYSICAL/MENTAL HEALTH ISSUES:

- #1 IN WORLDWIDE PRISON POPULATION: 2,121,600
- 20% OF ALL PRISONERS WORLDWIDE HELD IN UNITED STATES
- 83.4% RECIDIVISM RATE
- 1.2 TRILLION DOLLAR ANNUAL *INCARCERATION COST
- HEP C, HIV/AIDS RATE 3X HIGHER THAN POPULATION
- 300-400% GREATER SUICIDE RATE THAN GENERAL POPULATION

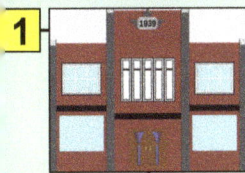

**1** | ESTABLISH PAK'S EDUCATION FOR QUALITY OF LIFE (E-QL) CIVILITY & KINDNESS PROGRAMS IN SCHOOLS STARTING AT 4 YEARS OLD & 1POP CLUBS THRU ADULTHOOD

**2** | GLOBAL EDUCATION & ACTION PROGRAMS FROM 16 THINGS SDG BOOKS & WORKSHOPS TO 30-DAY SIREM & SIREM SPEAKS EVENTS ON SOCIAL/INSTITUTIONAL REFORM

**3** | CAREER TRACK MANAGEMENT COURSES & INTERN/MENTORSHIPS COMBINE EDUCATION & REAL WORLD MANAGEMENT & LEADERSHIP TRAINING FOR YOUTH & ADULTS

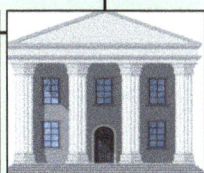

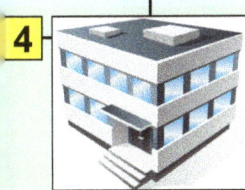

**4** | ONE PLANET INNOVATIONS CSR WORK/LIFE BALANCE CLIENT PROGRAMS FOR EMPLOYEES/FAMILIES INCLUDE PAK PROGRAMS: MANAGEMENT TRAINING; GREATER SAFETY/CASH ACCUMULATION FOR RETIREMENT, LTC COVERAGE, NO TAX W/D, ASSET PROTECTION; PROJECT KOPE HEALTH & WELLNESS; GLOBAL VOLUNTEER PROGRAMS

**PROACTIVE & PREVENTATIVE:** ESTABLISH THE PROGRAMS IN THE PRISON SYSTEM AS WELL WHERE THE SUM OF THESE PROGRAMS IS TO PROVIDE A QUALITY OF LIFE SUPPORT SYSTEM THAT'S DESPERATELY NEEDED

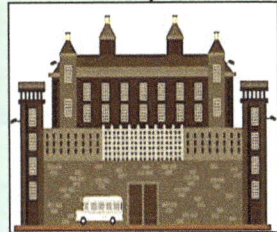

THE ADDITIONAL BENEFITS TO SOCIETY ARE:
- FEWER PEOPLE ENTERING/RETURNING TO PRISON
- LOWER GOVT EXPENDITURES/HIGHER TAX REVENUE
- IMPROVED POPULATION HEALTH & WELL-BEING
- SAFER COMMUNITIES • STRONGER FAMILIES
- LOWER DEATH, SUICIDE RATES

REDUCTION IN: GUN & DOMESTIC VIOLENCE; RACISM; RELIGIOUS, GENDER INTOLERANCE; SUBSTANCE ABUSE

*Author's Note: I was shocked when I understood that the cost of running the prisons is almost equal to the total cost of Medicare & Medicaid combined: 1.4 trillion

# COLLABORATION THINK TANK VOLUNTEERS

## WANTED: PROFESSIONALS • INDUSTRY EXPERTS • RETIREES • COLLEGE & GRAD STUDENTS

### BE THE HERO: PUT YOUR TALENT & HEART TOGETHER & BE PART OF THE SOLUTION

**OBJECTIVES:** • PREVENT GLOBAL TIPPING POINTS
• HELP PLANET ACHIEVE ALL 17 OF UNITED NATIONS SDGs
• IMPROVE QUALITY OF LIFE FOR KIDS, PEOPLE & THE PLANET

**REQUIREMENTS:**
4+ HOURS WEEKLY
3 MONTH MINIMUM

**APPLY ON APP**

### CHOOSE YOUR COLLABORATIVE VOLUNTEER PATH

**1 DATA & ANALYTICS**
CHOOSE SDG AREA(S) OF INTEREST, RESEARCH SUBJECTS, EXPERTS & DOCUMENT FINDINGS

**2 MEETINGS/EVENTS**
ESTABLISH & MANAGE MEETINGS BETWEEN EXPERTS & COLLABORATIVE PARTNERS

**3 MARKETING & PR**
PUBLICIZE PROGRAM & SOLUTIONS TO INSTITUTIONS IN COUNTRIES AROUND THE WORLD

**4 BUSINESS DEVELOP.**
CONTACT BUSINESSES REGARDING SPONSORSHIP OF SPECIFIC SDG RELATED PROGRAMS

### CHOOSE YOUR SUSTAINABLE DEVELOPMENT AREA(S) OF INTEREST

**1 2 NO POVERTY/HUNGER**

**3 HEALTH/WELLNESS**

**4 QUALITY EDUCATION**

**5 GENDER EQUALITY**

**6 CLEAN WATER**

**7 CLEAN ENERGY**

**8 DECENT WORK**

**9 11**
9. INDUSTRY INNOVATION INFRASTRUCTURE
11. SUSTAINABLE CITIES & COMMUNITIES

**10 REDUCED INEQUALITY**
WHY DO MOST GET PAID SO LITTLE? WHY DO SOME GET PAID TOO MUCH?

**12 RESPONSIBLE CONSUMPTION PRODUCTION**

**13 CLIMATE ACTION**

**14 LIFE BELOW WATER**

**15 LIFE ON LAND**

**16 PEACE & JUSTICE**

**17 IPOP INSTITUTION & INFLUENCER COLLABORATION THINK TANK NETWORK**

**PARTNERSHIPS GOALS**

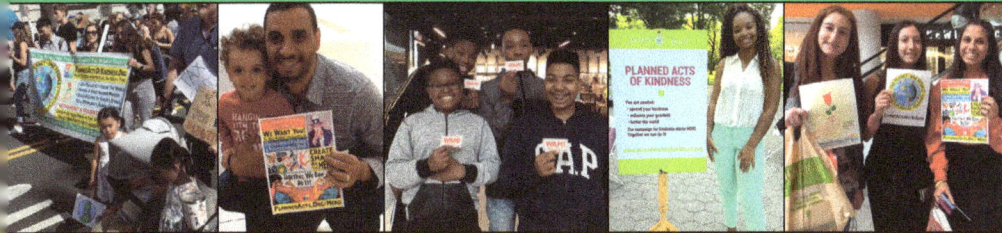

# CLIMATE CHANGE & YOU:
## FREEDOM OF CHOICE
### DOES NOT MEAN FREEDOM FROM CONSEQUENCES

**IF YOU THINK YOU'RE PART OF AN ORG OR BUSINESS IN THE U.S. THAT'S TOO BIG OR TOO SMALL TO COLLABORATE, HERE ARE A FEW REASONS WHY YOU'RE NOT. NEED MORE REASONS TO COLLABORATE? WE'VE GOT OVER SEVEN BILLION MORE.**

**1**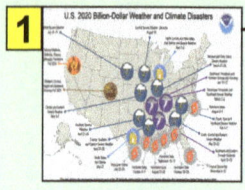

INCREASING NUMBER OF HURRICANES, SUPERSTORMS, TORNADOS, BLIZZARDS, SNOWSTORMS IMPACTING YOU, YOUR SUPPLIERS, CLIENTS, CUSTOMERS, PROSPECTS.
IMAGINE THE IMPACT OF 12-18 CRIPPLING EVENTS PER YEAR?

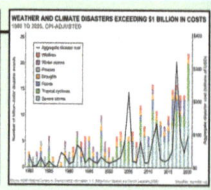

**2**

| HURRICANES: | YRS | LIVES AFFECTED | COST |
|---|---|---|---|
| 80 | 2017-2020 | N/A | $407,943,000,000 |
| 256 | 2000-2016 | N/A | $481,154,700,000 |

OUTLOOK: HURR. SEASON EXPANDS, U.S. STORMS INCREASE 3-FOLD CREATING HURRICANE CHAINS OF CONTINUOUS ACTIVITY DISPLACING OVER 1/3 OF POP

**3**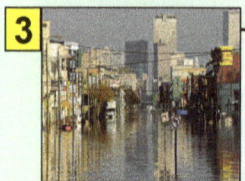

| FLOODS: | YEARS | LIVES AFFECTED | COST |
|---|---|---|---|
| 14 | 2018-2020 | 458,959,237 | N/A |
| 104 | 2000-2017 | 437,636,799 | N/A |

OUTLOOK: SEVEN FLOODS IN ONE YEAR COULD DISPLACE ONE BILLION PEOPLE, 3X'S THE U.S. POP. MEANING SOME GET HIT MULTIPLE TIMES

**4**

| ELECTRICITY: | YEARS | LIVES AFFECTED | COST |
|---|---|---|---|
| 17 | 2018-2020 | 65,572,000 | N/A |
| 51 | 2000-2017 | 160,703,500 | N/A |

OUTLOOK: EIGHT OUTAGES IN ONE YEAR WOULD AFFECT 174,800,000 PEOPLE (HALF THE U.S. POP). MEANING SOME GET HIT MULTIPLE TIMES

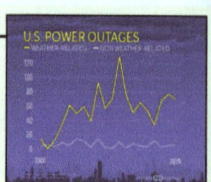

**5**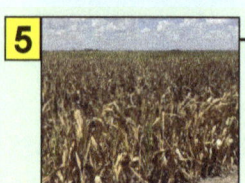

| DROUGHT: | YEARS | LIVES AFFECTED | COST |
|---|---|---|---|
| 25 | 2018-2020 | 127,173,306 | $2,599,080,000 |
| 86 | 2000-2017 | 839,959,200 | $25,112,670,000 |

OUTLOOK: DROUGHT, WATER SHORTAGES, CROP FAILURES, RESOURCE BATTLES POINT TO FUTURE WHERE WORST ENEMY IS US & CIVIL WAR

**6**

| FIRES: | YEARS | ACRES AFFECTED | COST |
|---|---|---|---|
| 167K | 2018-2020 | 23,554,192 | $103,991,000,000 |
| 1,246K | 2000-2017 | 106,226,023 | $349,153,000,000 |

OUTLOOK: INCREASING NUMBER OF FIRES, ACREAGE, LENGTH, DAMAGE IS DISRUPTIVE, COSTLY, HEALTH HAZARD & ENVIRONMENTAL DISASTER

California Megafires Rise with Increase in Global Heating

**THE TIME TO ACT IS NOW — CONTACT US TO LEARN HOW WE CAN COMBINE YOUR MISSION, YOUR CAUSE, YOUR OBJECTIVES WITH A COLLABORATION PLAN THAT WORKS FOR YOU AS WELL AS PEOPLE & THE PLANET.**

# THE 1POP COLLABORATION GUIDE IS THE "ONE" BOOK YOU HAVE TO HAVE

## SECTION IV:
## BE THE HERO

"WE CANNOT SEEK ACHIEVEMENT FOR OURSELVES AND FORGET ABOUT PROGRESS AND PROSPERITY FOR OUR COMMUNITY ... OUR AMBITIONS MUST BE BROAD ENOUGH TO INCLUDE THE ASPIRATIONS AND NEEDS OF OTHERS, FOR THEIR SAKES AND FOR OUR OWN."
— CESAR CHAVEZ

# You are Invited to HOST & POST The Daily Planned Acts of Kindness

## PAK
## PLANNED ACTS OF KINDNESS
### MAKING THE WORLD A BETTER PLACE, ONE PAK AT A TIME

PLANNED ACTS OF KINDNESS IS A GLOBAL OUTREACH PROGRAM WHERE PEOPLE WAKE UP AND ON THEIR CELL PHONE, COMPUTER OR DEVICE THERE IS A **NEW DAILY PLANNED ACT OF KINDNESS** THAT THEY CAN DO WITH THEIR FAMILY, FRIENDS, COWORKERS AND IN THEIR COMMUNITY.

# OUTREACH, ENGAGE & INSPIRE
# CONNECT & SHARE IN YOUR WORLD

TEXTS — **HOMES**
ASSEMBLY — **SCHOOLS**
ANNOUNCE — **FAITH-BASED**
WEBSITES — **NPOs/NGOs**
APPS — **COMPANIES**
WELLNESS — **GOVERNMENTS**
PROGRAMS?

THE GOAL IS TO HAVE TENS OF MILLIONS OF PEOPLE AROUND THE COUNTRY, HUNDREDS OF MILLIONS OF PEOPLE AROUND THE WORLD, WAKING UP AND DOING THE SAME PLANNED ACT OF KINDNESS ON THE SAME DAY, AND UNLEASHING THAT MUCH POWERFUL, POSITIVE ENERGY IN THE WORLD.

## THE WORLD NEEDS MORE HEROES

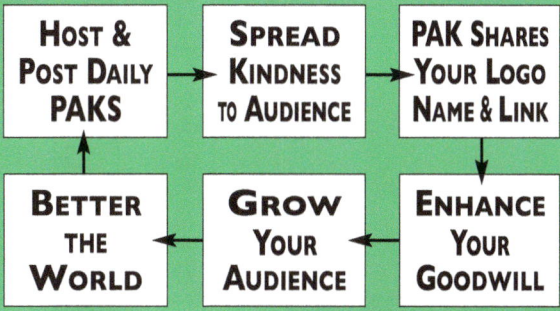

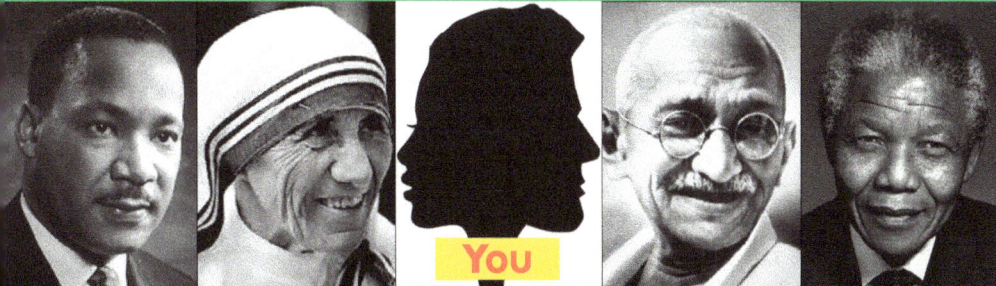

**HOST & POST DAILY PAKS** → **SPREAD KINDNESS TO AUDIENCE** → **PAK SHARES YOUR LOGO NAME & LINK** → **ENHANCE YOUR GOODWILL** → **GROW YOUR AUDIENCE** → **BETTER THE WORLD** → **HOST & POST DAILY PAKS**

YOU

"I hereby make a PAK to treat others with respect & kindness and to go through life from this day foreward acting towards others as I would wish to be treated myself."

| GET THE PAK APP | GO TO HOST & POST | SIGN-UP TO BE A HOST | CHOOSE POST TYPE | ON-LINE PRINT VERBAL | SHARE PAKs DAILY | PROMOTE MULTIPLE WAYS | PROVIDE US WITH YOUR LINK | WE ADD YOU TO APP |

# BE THE HERO! WE'RE ALL IN THIS TOGETHER

## IT DOESN'T MATTER HOW YOU ARE CONNECTED: IT MATTERS THAT YOU TAKE ACTION

**FOLLOW THE YELLOW BRICKS ...**

HOMES → NO MATTER WHO YOU ARE ... → EMPLOYEE/CONTRACTOR → YOU'RE MORE CONNECTED → CUSTOMER/MEMBER

SCHOOLS → SHARE THE ONE BOOK → NPOs/NGOs → OR SPECIFIC PROGRAMS → COMPANIES → WITH YOUR COMMUNITY

**SCHOOLS:**
STUDENTS & PARENTS
PRIMARY/ELEMENTARY SCHOOLS
JUNIOR/MIDDLE SCHOOLS
SENIOR/HIGH SCHOOLS
COMMUNITY COLLEGES
UNDERGRADUATE COLLEGES, UNIVERSITIES
GRADUATE SCHOOL MASTERS, PH.D PROGRAMS
SPECIALIZED DEGREES
HOME SCHOOL ASSOCIATIONS
CHARTER SCHOOLS
RELIGIOUS SCHOOLS
PREP SCHOOLS
MILITARY SCHOOLS
VOCATIONAL SCHOOLS
TRADE SCHOOLS
ADMINISTRATORS
TEACHERS, EDUCATORS, PROFESSORS
PRINCIPALS, DEPARTMENT CHAIRS
SUPERINTENDENTS, PRESIDENTS
SPORTS TEAMS, CLUBS, LEAGUES, DIVISIONS
CLUBS
FRATERNITIES, SORORITIES
PTOS
UNIONS
ASSOCIATIONS
TRADE ORGANIZATIONS

**CORPORATE PEOPLE OF INFLUENCE:**
CUSTOMERS, CLIENTS, MEMBERS, PROSPECTS
EMPLOYEES, CONTRACTORS, CONSULTANTS
MANAGERS, SUPERVISORS
DEPARTMENT & DIVISION HEADS
PRESIDENT, EXECUTIVES
CEO, C-SUITE
CHAIR & BOARD MEMBERS

**U.S. NON-PROFIT ORGANIZATIONS:**
501(C)(1) - ORG. BY ACT OF CONGRESS
501(C)(3) - CHARITABLE ORGANIZATIONS
501(C)(4) - CIVIC LEAGUE, SOCIAL WELFARE ORGS
501(C)(6) - TRADE OR PROFESSIONAL
501(C)(7) - SOCIAL OR RECREATIONAL CLUB
501(C)(10) - DOMESTIC FRATERNAL SOCIETIES & ASSOC.
501(C)(19) - VETERANS ORGANIZATIONS
501(D) - RELIGIOUS AND APOSTOLIC ASSOCIATIONS
501(E) - COOPERATIVE HOSPITAL SERVICE ORGS

> "It isn't enough to think outside the box. Thinking is passive. Get used to acting outside the box."
> — Tim Ferriss

**NON-GOVERNMENTAL ORGANIZATIONS:**
ADVOCACY NGOS & OPERATIONAL NGOS
BINGO - BUSINESS FRIENDLY INTERNATIONAL NGO
CITS - YOUTH DEVELOPMENT IN R&D FROM
   SCIENTIFIC COMMUNITY
CSO - CIVIL SOCIETY ORGANIZATION
DONGO - DONOR ORGANIZED NGO
ENGO - ENVIRONMENTAL NGO
GONGO - GOVERNMENT OPERATED NGO
GSO - GRASSROOTS SUPPORT ORGANIZATION
CHARDS - COMMUNITY HEALTH & RURAL
   DEVELOPMENT SOCIETY

**PEOPLE OF INFLUENCE:**
MEMBERS, ADMINISTRATORS, EXECUTIVES, FOUNDERS
DONORS, SUPPORTS, SPONSORS

**GLOBAL INFLUENCERS:** ATHLETES, CELEBS, ACTORS,
MUSICIANS, AUTHORS, ARTISTS, BANDS, PAINTERS, HEALERS,
COACHES, BLOGGERS, PODCASTERS, INTERNET INFLUENCERS

**COMPANIES/FRANCHISES**
ACCESSORIES
ACCOMMODATIONS
AIRLINES
AMUSEMENT PARKS
APPAREL
APPLIANCES
ARTS & CRAFTS
AUTOMAKERS
AUTOMOTIVE
BABY PRODUCTS
BANKS
BEAUTY
BEVERAGES
BOOKSTORES
BOX STORES
CHAIN STORES
CHEMICAL COMPANIES
CLOTHING
COMPUTERS
CONSTRUCTION
COURIERS
CRUISE LINES
DEPARTMENT STORES
DRUG STORES
E-COMMERCE
ELECTRIC COMPANIES
ELECTRONICS
ENTERTAINMENT
FAST FOOD CHAINS
FINANCIAL SERVICES
FOOD COMPANIES
FURNITURE
GAMES
GARDEN & LANDSCAPING
HAMBURGER FRANCHISES

HEALTH
HEALTHCARE
HOME GOODS
HOTELS
INSURANCE
INTERNET
INVESTMENT SERVICES
LEISURE
LUXURY GOODS
MALLS
MEDIA COMPANIES
MEDIA SERVICES
MOVIE THEATERS
MUSIC LABELS
MUSIC PLATFORMS
OFFICE SUPPLIES
OIL & GAS COMPANIES
OUTDOOR PRODUCTS
PET SUPPLIES
PHARMACEUTICALS
PIZZA FRANCHISES
PROFESSIONAL SERVICES
REAL ESTATE
RESORTS
RESTAURANT CHAINS
RETAILERS
SHOES & FOOT WARE
SOFTWARE DEVELOPERS
SPORTS TEAMS, LEAGUES
STUDIOS
TECHNOLOGY
TELECOMMUNICATIONS
TOURISM
TOYS
TRANSPORTATION
TRAVEL

WE SAID → "BE THE HERO" → WE SAID → "GETTING STARTED IS EASY" → SHARE THE ONE BOOK → WE DO THE HEAVY LIFTING → WHAT WE DIDN'T SAY WAS ...

# WE NEED YOUR HELP. YOUR CONNECTIONS & ACTIONS ARE WANTED!

## YOU MAY BE THE RIGHT PERSON AT THE RIGHT TIME TO MAKE IT HAPPEN: C + A = HERO

**ONE** — The Fight for Survival of the Human Race

By Lyle Benjamin with Alice Mok

Founder of One Planet One People, Planned Acts of Kindness & the Collaboration Think Tank Network

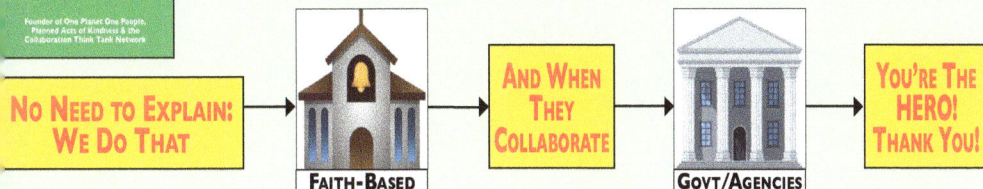

AND YOU ARE MORE POWERFUL → **STAKEHOLDER** → THAN YOU MIGHT THINK. → **SHAREHOLDER**

NO NEED TO EXPLAIN: WE DO THAT → **FAITH-BASED** → AND WHEN THEY COLLABORATE → **GOVT/AGENCIES** → YOU'RE THE HERO! THANK YOU!

---

**WHO DO YOU KNOW?**

**WHO ELSE CAN YOU REACH?**

**WHAT WILL YOU SHARE?**

**WHAT'S YOUR WEEKLY CONNECTION GOAL?**

**WHO DO YOU WANT TO BE THE HERO FOR?**

### FAITH-BASED ORGS:
Christianity
Islam
Hinduism
Jainism
Buddhism
Sikhism
Ethnic/Folk
Judaism
Religious Schools
Associations
Clubs
Youth Centers
Community Centers
Senior Centers
Missions
Charitable Events
Fund-Raising Programs
Social Programs
Literacy Programs
Educational Programs

#### PEOPLE OF INFLUENCE:
Congregants & Staff
Cardinals, Bishops
Fathers, Priests, Pastors
Imams, Emir, Mullah
Puhari, Archaka
Muni, Aryika
Lama, Bhikkhuni
Clergy, Ministers
Rabbis, Cantors

> "It's being relevant. Just alive & invested."
> — Michael J. Fox

### COMPANIES/FRANCHISES
Accessories
Accommodations
Airlines
Amusement Parks
Apparel
Appliances
Arts & Crafts
Automakers
Automotive
Baby Products
Banks
Beauty
Beverages
Bookstores
Box Stores
Chain Stores
Chemical Companies
Clothing
Computers
Construction
Couriers
Cruise Lines
Department Stores
Drug Stores
E-Commerce
Electric Companies
Electronics
Entertainment
Fast Food Chains
Financial Services
Food Companies
Furniture
Games
Garden & Landscaping
Hamburger Franchises

Health
Healthcare
Home Goods

#### PEOPLE OF INFLUENCE:
Constituents, Staff, Local, City, State, Fed. Employees, Contractors
Diplomats, Ambassadors
Mayors, Governors
Representatives, Senators
White House

Media Companies
Media Services
Movie Theaters
Music Labels
Music Platforms
Office Supplies
Oil & Gas Companies
Outdoor Products
Pet Supplies
Pharmaceuticals
Pizza Franchises
Professional Services
Real Estate
Resorts
Restaurant Chains
Retailers
Shoes & Foot Ware
Software Developers
Sports Teams, Leagues
Studios
Technology
Telecommunications
Tourism
Toys
Transportation
Travel

### GOVERNMENT/AGENCIES:
Admin for Children/Families
Admin for Community Living
Admin for Native Americans
Agency for Global Media
Agency for Intl Development
Bureau of Indian Affairs
Bureau of Land Management
Bureau of Ocean Energy Mgt
Bureau of Reclamation
Bureau of Safety & Environ-
    mental Enforcement
Children's Bureau
Corporation for National
    and Community Service
Department of Agriculture
Department of Commerce
Department of Education
Department of Energy
Department of Health and
    Human Services
Dept of Homeland Security
Department of Housing and
    Urban Development
Department of Justice
Department of Labor
Department of State
Department of the Interior
Department of the Treasury
Department of Transportation
Department of Veterans Affairs
Energy Information Admin
Environment and Natural
    Resources Division
Environ. Protection Agency
ESK National Institute Child

---

"THE MORE YOU DO → THE GREATER YOUR REWARDS!" → **PAK** → THE KARMA CLUB → EVERYTHING YOU DO COUNTS!!! → DAILY PAKs VOLUNTEER ENGAGEMENT SUPPORT → EARN YOUR REWARDS & BTH!

45

## RAPID RESPONSE TEAM ONE
RESEARCH • ACTION • PERSISTANT • INSISTANT • DELIVERABLES

**DUTIES: SOLVE PRESSING QUESTIONS FAST
WORK DIRECTLY WITH FOUNDER, LYLE BENJAMIN**

**SKILLS & ATTITUDES:**
CRACK RESEARCHER
COMPUTER WHIZ
SMOOTH COMMUNICATOR
QUICK STUDY
PRODIGIOUSLY PROACTIVE
PASSIONATE ABOUT PROCEDURES
BURNING DESIRE TO SUCCEED
STEELY DETERMINATION
*NEVER GIVE UP, NEVER SURRENDER
*BONUS POINTS FOR THIS ONE!

**APPLY Now!**

### HAVE EXPERIENCE IN:
- BUSINESS DEVELOPMENT?
- CROWD-FUNDING?
- FUND-RAISING?
- GRANT WRITING?
- SPONSORSHIPS?
- DONATIONS?
- SPECIAL EVENTS?

LOCAL, NATIONAL, GLOBAL

### HR PROS
RECRUIT
TRAIN
EVALUATE
MENTOR
VOLUNTEERS
INTERNS
WORKERS
MANAGERS
LEADERS

### DIGITAL & BRAND STRATEGISTS
### CREATIVE & ART DIRECTORS
### WEB & APP DEVELOPERS & DESIGNERS
### UX & UI DESIGNERS

### VOL. FOR CAAP
CRAZY AMBITIOUS ACTIVITIES PROGRAMS
GO SOLO OR GO TEAM

### TRANSLATORS TO BRING OUR MATERIAL & PROGRAMS TO LIFE FOR EVERY LANGUAGE

### EARN YOUR CPI CERTIFICATION
✓ CONSISTENCY
✓ PERSISTENCY
✓ INSISTENCY

### PROGRAMMERS, CODERS FOR WEB SITES APPLICATIONS GAMES & SOFTWARE

### "BE THE HERO" ACTIVISTS WANTED
to START, MANAGE & LEAD
ONE PLANET ONE PEOPLE CLUBS
IN SCHOOLS & COMMUNITIES
AROUND THE WORLD

---

### LOCATE THE VOLUNTEER PROGRAMS ON THE
## PAK APP
**SIGN-UP & FOLLOW the START-UP STEPS**

### PROJECT MANAGERS & DIRECTORS
WANTED FOR PAK & 1POP BOOKS, PROGRAMS, INITIATIVES AROUND THE WORLD

### TEACHERS, EDUCATORS, SCHOOL STAFF & ADMINISTRATORS
PROMOTE HEALTHY LEARNING ENVIRONMENTS, POSITIVE SUPPORT SYSTEMS & RELATIONSHIPS. REDUCE ANXIETY, STRESS, BULLYING, NEGATIVE INFLUENCES, SELF ABUSE & SUICIDE.

- E-QL: DAILY PLANNED ACTS OF KINDNESS
- 1POP CLUBS: REAL WORLD ENGAGEMENT
- CAAP: CRAZY AMBITIOUS ACTIVITIES PROGRAM
- PROJECT KOPE: HEALTH, HAPPINESS, WELLNESS
- INTERNSHIP/MENTORSHIP PROGRAM
- CAREER TRACK MANAGEMENT PROGRAM

### COLLABORATION THINK TANK VOLS
PROFESSIONALS • INDUSTRY EXPERTS
RETIREES • COLLEGE & GRAD STUDENTS

DATA & ANALYTICS   MARKETING/PR
BUSINESS DEVELOP   MEETINGS/EVENTS

WORKING WITH INSTITUTIONS TO:
- HELP PREVENT THE TIPPING POINTS
- HELP ACHIEVE ALL 17 U.N. SDGs
- HELP IMPROVE QUALITY OF LIFE

8+ VOLUNTEER HOURS MONTHLY • 3 MONTH MIN.

### ATHLETES, COACHES & EXECS.
AMATEUR, PRO, RETIRED

DO HAVE A PASSION, CAUSE OR MISSION? OR DO YOU LIKE OURS?

FIND OUT WHAT WE CAN DO TO BRING QUALITY OF LIFE TO MILLIONS

ALSO BRING OUR MENTORSHIP, FINANCE & CAREER TRACK MANAGEMENT PROGRAMS INTO COLLEGES & LEAGUES

---

### COOKS WANTED ONE TABLE ONE WORLD

### BECOME A GLOBAL PEACE AMBASSADOR
GOOD WITH PEOPLE? OUTREACH & ENGAGE. BUILD & MANAGE A TEAM. COLLABORATE USING CAMPAIGNS, CHALLENGES, PROGRAMS & INITIATIVES
BE THE INSPIRATION TO THOUSANDS OR MILLIONS: IT'S ALL UP TO YOU!

### VOLS FOR CAUSES
ABUSE
AGING
BULLYING
CIVILITY
CLIMATE
DRUGS
EDUCATION
ENERGY
ENVIRONMENT
ETHICS
EQUALITY
FOOD/WATER
FINANCE
GENDER
HEALTH/WELL.
HOMELESSNESS
KINDNESS
MENTAL HEALTH
NUTRITION
PANDEMICS
POLLUTION
POVERTY
RACISM
RELIGION
RETIREMENT
SAFETY
SUSTAINABILITY
VIOLENCE
WORK CSR

### SOCIAL MEDIA WIZARDS WANTED!
- TIKTOKKERS
- BLOGGSTERS
- FACEBOOK LIVERS?!
- PODCASTINGERS
- INSTAGRAMMIES
- REEDITERS
- TWITTERERS
- WECHATTERS
- LINKEDINSIDERS
- WHATSAPPSTERS

**CREATE & RUN GLOBAL CAMPAIGNS!**

**GET SELECTED & FEATURED ON PAK OR 1POP SPECIALS!**

### ARTISTS, ILLUSTRATORS, ANIMATORS, VISUAL COMMUNICATIONS
### VOCALISTS, LYRICISTS, MUSICIANS
### DANCERS, PERFORMERS, ACTORS, MODELS

### MEETING PLANNERS
EVENT PLANNERS
PARTY PLANNERS
SPECIAL EVENT PLANNERS
CONFERENCE PLANNERS
EXHIBITION PLANNERS
TRADE SHOW PLANNERS
ASSOCIATION PLANNERS
DESTINATION PLANNERS
TRAVEL & HOSPITALITY PLANNERS
AND YES, EVEN
WEDDING PLANNERS*
*WITH PLANNED ACTS OR 1POP THEMES

### OGW EduMart
ENGINEERS
ARCHITECTS
CONTRACTORS
DEVELOPERS

### BAKERS, COOKS & CHEFS OH MY!

### BROADCAST, PRINT & DIGITAL JOURNALISTS, WRITERS, BLOGGERS, PODCASTERS
### EDITORS, PROOF READERS GRAPHIC DESIGNERS, DESKTOP PUBLISHERS
### COPYWRITERS MARKETERS, PUBLICISTS

---

**FIND YOUR PASSION** → **FEEL YOUR PASSION** → **FOLLOW YOUR PASSION** → **FEED YOUR PASSION** → **FUEL YOUR PASSION** → **FUN/D YOUR PASSION** → **FREE YOUR PASSION**

# Mini Bucket List of Company Collaborations
## Help Fast Track Quality of Life Outcomes By Creating Win-Win-Wins

**BRANDED BULK BOOKS**
EXHANCE YOUR MISSION, MESSAGE REPUTATION & REV. EXPONENTIALLY MKTG., ADV., PR, CSR & SALES

FEATURES:
CEO ON COVER, BOOK INTRO CHAPTER ON COMPANY
FULL COLOR MULTI-PAGE SPREAD
MULTIPLE MARKETS, MULTIPLE TITLES:
PLANNED ACTS OF KINDNESS; ONE
16 THINGS BOOKS & WORKSHOPS
THE WORKING DEAD
LEGACY LIFELINES MEMORIAL BOOKS

**NPOs, NGOs & FAITH-BASED ORGS**
WE ARE HERE TO HELP SUPPORT YOUR MISSIONS & VISIONS.

WE CAN HELP WITH FUND-RAISING.

WE HAVE INSPIRATIONAL YOUTH PROGRAMS TO COMPLIMENT YOURS.

WE CAN PROVIDE GLOBAL QUALITY OF LIFE EDUCATION, HEALTH & INCOME PROGRAMS.

**HEALTH & WELLNESS PROGRAMS & INITIATIVES**
FOR EMPLOYEES & CONTRACTORS WITH FAMILY OPTIONS: BENEFITS, CSR, TEAM-BUILDING, VOLUNTEER

**MEDIA, ORGS & WEB-SITE OWNERS ADD PAK's HOST & POST PROGRAM** TO SHARE DAILY PLANNED ACTS OF KINDNESS
WITH USERS, MEMBERS, AUDIENCE & CUSTOMERS AS WAY TO DEMONSTRATE CORPORATE SOCIAL RESPONSIBILITY

**GLOBAL GOVERNMENTS**
THE TIME HAS COME WHEN WE MUST PUT ASIDE OUR DIFFERENCES AS NATIONS AND WORK TOGETHER AS **ONE PLANET ONE PEOPLE** WITH A COMMON VISION & MISSION: QUALITY OF LIFE FOR ALL.

PLEASE DON'T HESITATE TO HAVE OFFICIALS IN YOUR ADMINISTRATION & THE UNITED NATIONS CONTACT US ON ANY ISSUE RELATED TO THE U.N. SUSTAINABLE DEVELOPMENT GOALS.

**GOVTS. & MAJOR SPONSORS**
E-QL IN SCHOOLS

**SPONSORS** FOR **U.S.** OR **GLOBAL**
1POP CLUBS

**SCHOOLS COLLEGES UNIVERSITIES**
ADD OUR CMTY. SERVICE, INTERNSHIP/ MENTORSHIP, CAREER TRACK, HEALTH & WELLNESS PROGRAMS

**TECH. & SOFTWARE CO's.**
WE NEED TO BORROW A FEW PROGRAMMERS, COMMANDEER SOME EQUIPMENT

HELP LAUNCH THREE GLOBAL PROGRAMS TO CONNECT, UNITE INSPIRE ACTION:

GLOBAL CLIMATE ACTION
FINANCIAL EQUALITY
COMMUNICATION

**FUND VETERAN TRAINING & WORK PROGRAMS**

**COMPANY SABBATICAL?**
COME ON-BOARD & BE THE HERO

**BOOST YOUR CSR THRU GROUND-BREAKING HR RECRUIT/RETAIN. PROGRAMS**
NO MATTER YOUR SIZE, OUR EXCLUSIVE PROGRAMS WILL SAVE YOU MONEY.
IF YOU THINK YOU CAN'T AFFORD IT, YOU OWE IT TO YOUR EMPLOYEES & TO YOUR COMPANY TO CONTACT US.
ALSO DISCUSS HOW TO EARN INCOME THRU OUR COLLABORATION NETWORK.

**PRODUCTS & GOODS DONATED TO PLANNED ACTS**
USED FOR PROMOTIONS AS WELL AS KARMA CLUB GIVE-AWAYS FOR MEMBERS THAT HAVE LEVELED-UP & BEEN SELECTED TO EARN THEIR KARMIC REWARDS

**CIVIC & SERVICE CLUBS**
COLLABORATE ON YOUR MISSION WITH PAK & 1POP PROGRAMS
ROTARY • KIWANIS • LIONS
KEY • APEX • ALTRUSA INTL
JCI • CIVITAN INTL • SERTOMA
EXCHANGE • OPTIMISTS
SOROPTIMISTS • ZONTA
QUOTA • BOYS & GIRLS CLUBS
SCOUTS • YMCA & YWCA

**SCHOOLS & UNIVERSITIES AGREE TO INTEGRATE**
PAK & 1POP COLLABORATIVE DISCIPLINE REAL WORLD EDUCATIONAL PROGRAMS INTO THE CURRICULUM GIVING STUDENTS THE OPPORTUNITY FOR THEIR CLASSWORK TO HAVE A POSITIVE IMPACT IN THE WORLD

**PAK LOGO PLACED IN MEDIA BUYS MEDIA TIME FOR PAK/1POP PSAs**

**AIRLINES & HOTELS**
ESTABLISH MILLION MILES REWARDS ACCOUNTS FOR PLANNED ACTS OF KINDNESS & ONE PLANET ONE PEOPLE TO FACILITATE DEVELOPMENT OF PROGRAMS & INITIATIVES

CONNECTIONS: C-SUITE, CSR, PR, MARKETING, ADVERTISING, BRANDING, SPECIAL EVENTS & SPONSORSHIPS

BENEFITS: INCREASED ENGAGEMENT WITH ACTIVIST AUDIENCE THAT SUPPORT COMPANIES THAT SUPPORT THEIR CAUSE

**TEAM-BUILDING, RECOGNITION & REWARDS THRU KINDNESS VOLUNTEER ACTIVITIES**

**COMPANIES** w/ **GREEN PRODUCTS**
COME JOIN OUR OGW EduMART

**ATTN: HR EMPLOYEES STUDENTS**
REDUCE:
ANXIETY
DEPRESSION
& SUICIDE
INCREASE:
HAPPINESS
HEALTH
WELLNESS
**PROJECT KOPE**

**APPAREL COMPANY**
TO LAUNCH
PAK & 1POP CLOTHING LINES

**NPR SPOTS**
WANTED FOR OUTREACH ENGAGEMENT & ACTION.
CAN PIGGYBACK ON EXISTING RADIO OR WEB

**SPONSOR KINDNESS PLEDGE CAMPAIGN** TO ADD MILLIONS TO WORLD VIDEO MAP

**FRANCHISES & CHAINS**
CUSTOM BENEFIT PROGRAMS
ENABLE YOUR FRANCHISEES TO:
1) RECRUIT & RETAIN BETTER PERSONNEL AT LOWER COST
2) EARN MORE REVENUE WHICH INCREASES YOUR BOTTOM LINE
3) GIVES YOU A COMPETITIVE ADVANTAGE ENABLING YOU TO SELL MORE FRANCHISES

**COMBINE WITH CUSTOM BOOK PROGRAM FOR EXCEPTIONAL BENEFITS**

**CSR SPONSORS WANTED FOR LEGACY LIFELINES MEMORIAL BRANDED BOOK GIVE-AWAY**
GOAL IS TO GIVE A FREE BOOK TO EVERY FAMILY THAT A LOST LOVED ONE DUE TO COVID-19 TO HELP THEM KEEP THE JOY AND MEMORIES OF THEIR LOVE ONE ALIVE FOR THEMSELVES, THEIR FAMILY AND FUTURE GENERATIONS

**PIZZA COMPANIES RISE UP! SPONSOR THE GREAT PIZZA PEACE PLAN CHALLENGE!**
BOOK, PROGRAM, WEB-SITE, APP, SOCIAL MEDIA, LIVE PROMOS. MULTI-YEAR TIE-INS. YOU'LL HAVE COMPANY ACING DELIVERIES

**PUBLIC RELATIONS FIRMS**
CAN TAKE ON PAK OR 1POP AS PRO BONO CLIENTS OR AGREE TO PROMOTE SPECIFIC PROGRAMS, INITIATIVES CAMPAIGNS OR CHALLENGES

**LIBRARIES: WE HAVE BOOKS, WORKSHOPS & COURSES. OH MY!**
LET'S WORK TOGETHER TO BRING KIDS & ADULTS ON-BOARD TO LEARN & TAKE ACTION TO BENEFIT QUALITY OF LIFE

**COMPANIES, ORGANIZATIONS & GOVERNMENTS WITH GROUND FLOOR SPACE**
(2,500 SQ. FT. - 15,000 SQ. FT)
FREE FOR PLANNED ACTS TO ESTABLISH COMMUNITY PARTNERSHIP CENTERS TO PROVIDE A WIDE RANGE OF FREE & LOW-COST QUALITY OF LIFE PROGRAMS & SERVICES TO ALL AREA RESIDENTS

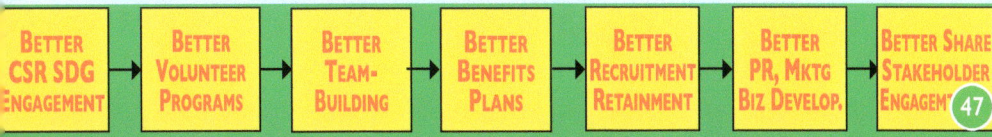

---

**BETTER CSR SDG ENGAGEMENT** → **BETTER VOLUNTEER PROGRAMS** → **BETTER TEAM-BUILDING** → **BETTER BENEFITS PLANS** → **BETTER RECRUITMENT RETAINMENT** → **BETTER PR, MKTG BIZ DEVELOP.** → **BETTER SHARE STAKEHOLDER ENGAGEM'T**

# INCOME & OPPORTUNITY UNCLASSIFIED BOARD

## WHAT GOES AROUND COMES AROUND • WE HELP TURN YOUR PASSION INTO PROFIT

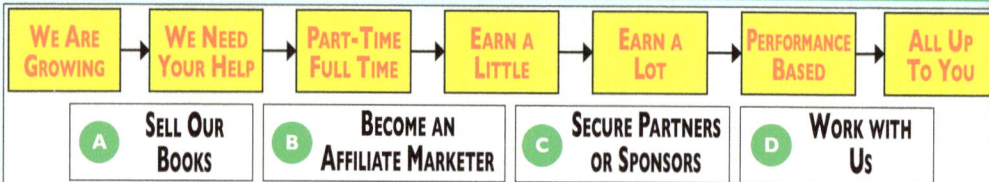

| WE ARE GROWING | → | WE NEED YOUR HELP | → | PART-TIME FULL TIME | → | EARN A LITTLE | → | EARN A LOT | → | PERFORMANCE BASED | → | ALL UP TO YOU |

**A** SELL OUR BOOKS   **B** BECOME AN AFFILIATE MARKETER   **C** SECURE PARTNERS OR SPONSORS   **D** WORK WITH US

**ALL COUNTRIES. ALL BACKGROUNDS. ALL WELCOME: STUDENTS • EMPLOYEES • OWNERS • RETIREES • UNEMPLOYED**
NO WHERE WILL YOU FIND MORE MEANINGFUL WAYS TO CONNECT TO SO MANY WITH SUCH AN INSPIRATIONAL IMPACT

**Q: WHY ME? WHY NOW?** **A: BECAUSE PEOPLE ALL OVER ARE SUFFERING & IT'S GOING TO GET WORSE. KINDNESS/COLLABORATION ARE THE ONLY SOLUTIONS & TIME IS RUNNING OUT.**

**Q: WHY US? A: CHECK YOURSELF**

- ☐ ORG MAKES A POSITIVE DIFFERENCE
- ☐ ORG'S VALUES ALIGN WITH YOURS
- ☐ ORG VALUES FAMILY & COMMUNITY
- ☐ WORK BRINGS YOU SATISFACTION
- ☐ YOU'LL FEEL APPRECIATED/VALUED
- ☐ WORK IS WHAT YOU'D LOVE TO DO
- ☐ WORK FITS YOUR PERSONALITY
- ☐ WORK BRINGS BALANCE TO LIFE
- ☐ WORK CHALLENGES YOU TO GROW

**A** SELL OUR BOOKS: ALL TYPES OF STORES, SCHOOLS, LIBRARIES, FAITH-BASED, NPOS, COMPANIES, GOVT • LOCAL NATL GLOBAL

OUR BOOKS HELP YOU BE THE HERO

| SOCIAL RESPONSIBILITY | 16 THINGS ... | CUSTOMIZED ... | SPECIAL EDITIONS | FINANCIAL LITERACY | HAPPINESS & WELLNESS |

**B** BECOME AN AFFILIATE MARKETER: SHARE YOUR AFFILIATE LINKS THRU SOCIAL MEDIA, BLOGS & WEBSITES

| PROGRAMS | BOOKS | COURSES | GET PAK APP | ACTIVITIES | EVENTS | GAMES |

**C** SECURE PARTNERS OR SPONSORS: SHARE YOUR AFFILIATE LINKS THRU SOCIAL MEDIA, BLOGS & WEBSITES

| DOZENS OF PROGRAMS & INITIATIVES | BOOK BRANDING PACKAGES FROM 250 TO 100,000 | CAREER TRACK MANAGEMENT COURSES | STUDENT ACTIVITIES FROM 4 YRS TO ADULT | WORKSHOPS, PUBLIC SPEAKING, SUMMITS | CUSTOM BOARD GAME DEVELOP. & PRODUCTION |

**D** WORK WITH US: MAKE YOUR LEGACY & HELP BRING QUALITY OF LIFE TO PEOPLE AROUND THE WORLD (+ BENEFITS!)

| BUSINESS DEV | PROJECT MGT | MARKETING PR | HUMAN RES. | FUNDRAISING | EDUCATION | SUSTAINABILITY | FINAN. ADVISOR | LTC BENEFITS |

# SECTION V:
# PROGRAMS & INITIATIVES

"THE LAW OF KARMA IS ALSO CALLED THE LAW OF CAUSE AND EFFECT, ACTION AND REACTION AND: AS YOU SOW, SO SHALL YOU REAP."
— SHAM HINDUJA

# The Karma Constitution

## Article I.

We the Children of the World Unite under One Planet One People in Order to Preserve, Protect, Nurture and Grow the Health of Our Planet and Our Global Community; and, do ordain and establish this Karma Constitution for Quality of Life for All.

Section 1.    Planned Acts of Kindness is hereby designated as the Global Organization for Supporters of the Karma Constitution. Supporters of the Karma Constitution become Members of the The Karma Club whereby they officially become active Members of Humanity.

Section 2.    Joining the Karma Club is, and always will be, free and open to all the Children of the World regardless of nationality, race, religion, color, gender, age, social, education, or economic condition.

Section 3.    Members of the Karma Club are encouraged to make a recording of themselves reciting the PAK Civility Pledge in what-ever language they speak: "I hereby make a PAK to treat others with respect & kindness and to go through life from this day forward acting towards others as I would wish to be treated myself."

Section 4.    Members of the Karma Club are encouraged to share their recording on the World Video Map and distribute it through Social Media platforms for all the world to see.

## Article II.

Members of the Karma Club are encouraged to perform four different types of activities during the course of each month. Members that perform the requisite number of achievements in all four activities can move up to the next Karmic level where they are then eligible to receive recognition and rewards.

Section 1.    Daily Planned Acts: Members of the Karma Club are encouraged to take action for the benefit of their family, friends, co-workers and community by completing and sharing their finished Planned Acts of Kindness on a daily basis.

Section 2.    Engagement: Members of the Karma Club are encouraged to inspire others to take action by having them join the Karma Club and take the PAK Pledge.

Section 3.    Volunteering: Members of the Karma Club are encouraged to show their commitment to the Bettering the World by Volunteering and taking part in Planned Acts & One Planet One People programs around the world.

Section 4.    Support: Members of the Karma Club are encouraged to Support Planned Acts & One Planet One People initiatives by securing donations, sponsorships and grants.

## Article III.

Members of the Karma Club are encouraged to join Planned Acts of Kindness' Global One Planet One People Social Responsibility Club (One Planet One People Club) and participate in Planned Acts' Volunteer Initiatives on either a local, national or global scale.

Section 1.    Joining a One Planet One People Club is open to all the Children of the World regardless of nationality, race, religion, color,

# One Planet One People

gender, age, social, education, health or economic condition.

Section 2.    Anyone who is a member of the Global One Planet One People Club can establish a community or institutional One Planet One People Club on a local, national or global scale by adhering to the policies and procedures established for Club operation by Planned Acts of Kindness.

Section 3.    Members of the One Planet One People Club are encouraged to use their interests and backgrounds to outreach, engage, inspire others to participate in Planned Acts of Kindness and One Planet One People education and action programs.

Section 4.    All One Planet One People Clubs, executives and members are required to faithfully follow the policies and procedures set forth by Planned Acts of Kindness and the Global One Planet One People Club as they work for the betterment of people and the planet.

## Article IV.

Section 1.    The Executive Power shall be vested in an Executive Director of the Karma Club and One Planet One People Club, who shall be one and the same individual as the Chief Executive Officer of Planned Acts of Kindness, Inc.

Section 2.    The Executive Director shall have the duty and responsibility to ratify One Planet One People Clubs around the World.

Section 3.    All One Planet One People Club Executives shall serve under a Memorandum of Understanding that defines the duties and responsibilities of their office and their agreement to actively work on fulfilling the mission and vision of Planned Acts of Kindness.

## Article V.

Section 1.    Members of the Karma Club are encouraged to build connections with others in the Global Community to further the mission and vision of the Karma Club, the One Planet One People Movement and Planned Acts of Kindness.

Section 2.    Members of the Karma Club are encouraged to submit new ideas and proposals with the objective of furthering the mission and vision of the Karma Club, the One Planet One People Movement and Planned Acts of Kindness

## Article VI.

This Constitution, and the Principles contained herein shall be made in Pursuance thereof; and all Treaties made, or which shall be made, under the Authority of the Children of the World, shall be the supreme Law of the Land; and the Members in every Community shall be bound thereby, anything in the Constitution or Laws of any Nation to the Contrary notwithstanding.

Done by the Unanimous Consent of the Members present in the Months of January in the Year of our Lord Two Thousand and Two in Witness whereof We have hereunto subscribed our Names:

Lyle Benjamin, Founder,
Planned Acts of Kindness, One Planet One People

ROBERT ADAMO, JACQUE ZOCCOLI, COUMBA
— VISIT PAK APP FOR ADDITIONAL SIGNEES —

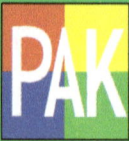 # THE KARMA CLUB
## THE MORE YOU DO, THE GREATER YOUR REWARDS

## PLANNED ACTS OF KINDNESS • "BE THE HERO" & JOIN US TODAY

THE KARMA CLUB PROVIDES INDIVIDUALS & ORGS A GLOBAL SOCIAL RESPONSIBILITY SYSTEM THAT WORKS TO "MAKE THE WORLD A BETTER PLACE, ONE PAK AT A TIME"

### THE KARMA CLUB'S FOUR MONTHLY ACTIVITIES: THE MORE YOU DO, THE GREATER YOUR REWARDS

**DAILY PLANNED ACTS**

**ENGAGEMENT**

**VOLUNTEERISM**

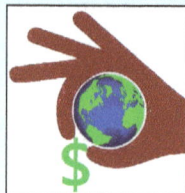
**SUPPORT**

### THE KARMA CLUB WORKS WITH 5 GROUPS OF PEOPLE & 5 TYPES OF ORGANIZATIONS IN ALIGNMENT WITH THE FOUR PILLARS OF THE ONE PLANET ONE PEOPLE MOVEMENT & THE UNITED NATIONS 17 SDGS

**ONE PLANET ONE PEOPLE:**
BASED ON THE PRINCIPLES OF
- CIVILITY
- SOCIAL RESPONSIBILITY
- VOLUNTEERISM
- GLOBAL CITIZENSHIP

**HELPING 5 GROUPS OF PEOPLE:**
- STUDENTS
- EMPLOYEES
- OWNERS
- RETIREES
- UNEMPLOYED

BY COLLABORATING WITH

**5 TYPES OF INSTITUTIONS:**
- SCHOOLS
- FAITH BASED ORGS
- NPOS / NGOS
- GOVERNMENTS
- BUSINESSES

**GOAL 1**
THE KARMA CLUB & ONE PLANET ONE PEOPLE MOVEMENT IN 200+ COUNTRIES WITH TENS OF MILLIONS OF PEOPLE AROUND THE WORLD DOING THE SAME PAK ON THE SAME DAY & UNLEASHING THAT MUCH POSITIVE, POWERFUL ENERGY INTO THE WORLD

**GOAL 2**
HAVE MEMBERS OF THE KARMA CLUB COLLABORATE ON COMMON CAUSES WITH A COMMON PURPOSE: STOPPING THE MAJOR PROBLEMS OF THE WORLD FROM REACHING THEIR TIPPING POINTS & NEGATIVELY AFFECTING THE QUALITY OF LIFE OF BILLIONS OF PEOPLE ON THE PLANET

**CLIMATE CHANGE**

**POLLUTION**

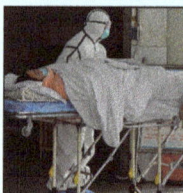
**PANDEMICS**

**WAR**

### PROGRAMS THAT INCORPORATE DAILY PLANNED ACTS OF KINDNESS & THE KARMA CLUB FOR ENGAGEMENT & ACTION

| THE KARMA CLUB | ONE PLANET ONE PEOPLE CLUBS | PROJECT KOPE WELLNESS PROGRAM |
|---|---|---|

THE KARMA CLUB CHALLENGE & REWARD COINS

# PAK

# EDUCATION FOR QUALITY OF LIFE

## E-QL QUALITY OF LIFE THRU PLANNED ACTS OF KINDNESS

# TO SOLVE THE PROBLEMS OF THE WORLD WE NEED TO ENGAGE & INSPIRE YOUTH OF ALL AGES

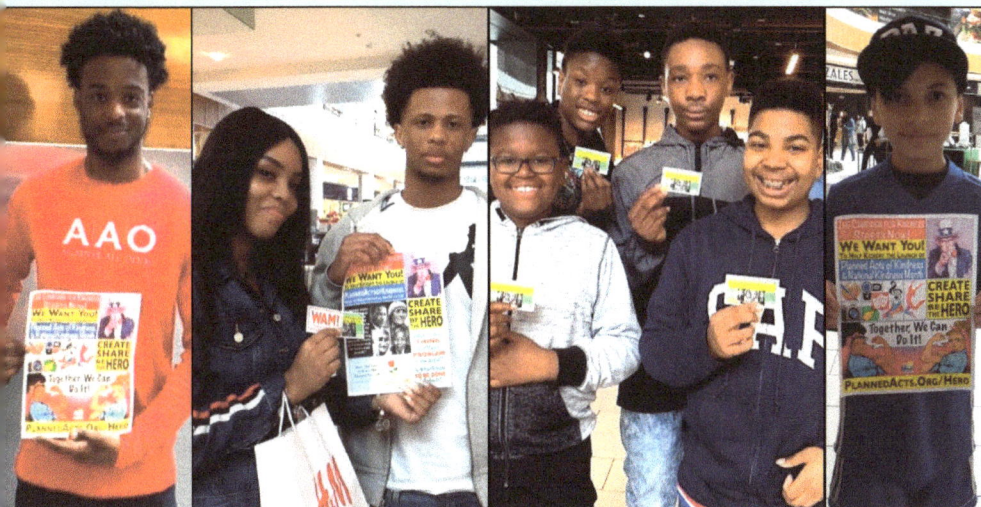

EDUCATION & ACTION PROGRAMS DESIGNED TO ENGAGE & INSPIRE BASED ON THE FOUR PILLARS OF "ONE PLANET ONE PEOPLE" — CIVILITY, SOCIAL RESPONSIBILITY, VOLUNTEERISM & GLOBAL CITIZENSHIP — TEACHING KINDNESS, DIVERSITY, INCLUSION & RESPONSIBILITY THROUGH LIFE SKILLS

---

### PATH 1 — EDUCATION FOR QUALITY OF LIFE (E-QL)

**OBJECTIVES:** PROVIDING YOUTH WITH 5-MINUTE ACTIVITIES THEY CAN DO IN SCHOOL (AND WITH FAMILY & FRIENDS) TO ACHIEVE RECOGNITION & REWARDS BASED ON POSITIVE BEHAVIOR

#### MONTHLY MASTER CALENDAR

4-8 YEARS: DAILY PLANNED ACTS OF KINDNESS
9-12 YEARS: DAILY PAKS & ART, MUSIC, DANCE, GLOBAL CITIZENS
13-17 YEARS: DAILY PAKS; A.M.D.; GC, V., IPOP CLUBS, INTERNS
18-26 YEARS: DAILY PAKS; A.M.D.; GC, V., INTERNS, CAREER TRACK

- CIVILITY & KINDNESS
- EQUALITY OF LIFE FOR ALL
- HEALTH & WELL-BEING
- SOCIAL JUSTICE
- GENDER/RACIAL TOLERANCE
- COLLABORATION SKILLS
- GLOBAL ISSUES

---

BE THE HERO! HELP BRING E-QL INTO SCHOOLS AROUND THE WORLD!

| 2022-25 GOALS | 200+ COUNTRIES | 100'S OF MILLIONS ENGAGED | 53 |

# ONE PLANET ONE PEOPLE CLUBS
## WORKING FOR E-QUALITY OF LIFE THROUGH PLANNED ACTS OF KINDNESS

# WE NEED YOUR HELP. WE NEED YOUR SUPPORT
## IN BUILDING ONE PLANET ONE PEOPLE CLUBS AROUND THE WORLD

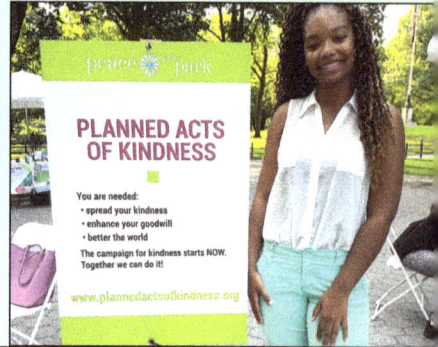

## CLUBS PROVIDE EDUCATION & ACTION PROGRAMS FULLY ALIGNED WITH THE 17 U.N. SDGS IN COLLABORATION WITH 5 TYPES OF INSTITUTIONS BENEFITING 5 GROUPS OF PEOPLE IN THE GLOBAL COMMUNITY

| CLUBS | BOOKS | COURSES | PROGRAMS | EVENTS | GAMES |
|-------|-------|---------|----------|--------|-------|

### PATH 2 — ONE PLANET ONE PEOPLE (1POP) CLUBS

**OBJECTIVES:** TO PROVIDE YOUTH WITH A SUPPORT PROGRAM THAT HELPS THEM BUILD QUALITY RELATIONSHIPS, SKILLS AND A STRONG SENSE OF COMMUNITY WHILE DOING ENGAGING ACTIVITIES THAT PROVIDE QUALITY OF LIFE FOR PEOPLE AROUND THE WORLD REGARDLESS OF NATIONALITY, RACE, RELIGION, AGE, GENDER, EDUCATION OR INCOME.

- THE KARMA CLUB: KARMA GAMIFIED
- BOOKS/WORKSHOPS/COURSES
- CRAZY AMBITIOUS ACTIVITIES
- INTERNSHIPS/MENTORSHIPS
- PROJECT KOPE WELLNESS PROGRAM
- SIREM: SOCIAL INSTITUTIONAL REFORM
- CAREER TRACK MANAGEMENT

## BE THE HERO! HELP BRING 1POP CLUBS IN COMMUNITIES AROUND THE WORLD!

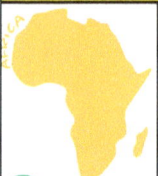

| AFRICA | ASIA | OCEANIA | EUROPE | N. AMERICA | S. AMERICA |
|--------|------|---------|--------|------------|------------|

# CLUB MAGAZINE & VIDEO PROGRAM
## DIGITAL PROGRAMS FEATURING MEMBERS TO ENGAGE & INSPIRE ACTION

## PEOPLE JOIN ONE PLANET ONE PEOPLE CLUBS
### BECAUSE THEY CARE ABOUT OTHERS & THEY CARE ABOUT THE PLANET

**ACTION**

| CLUBS CONTAIN THE PROGRAMS & INITIATIVES OF IPOP & PAK | MEMBERS CHOOSE PROGRAMS BASED ON THEIR INTERESTS | MEMBERS GET TO DEVELOP & USE THEIR SKILLS WHILE MAKING AN IMPACT |

ART • ANIMATION • APP DEVELOPMENT • BROADCASTING • BUSINESS • COMPUTERS • DANCE • DESIGN • EVENTS • GRAPHICS • JOURNALISM

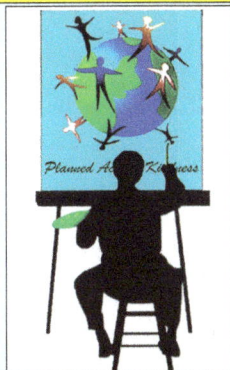

LEADERSHIP • MANAGEMENT • MARKETING • MERCHANDISING • PROGRAMMING • PROMOTIONS • SOCIAL MEDIA • SPORTS • VIDEO PRODUCTION

**DEVELOP**

| REAL WORLD OUTREACH, ENGAGEMENT, INSPIRATION & ACTION LOCAL • NAT'L • GLOBAL | IMPACTS QUALITY OF LIFE FOR MEMBERS, PEOPLE & THE PLANET. TEACHES HOW TO "BE THE HERO" | ACKNOWLEDGES & REWARDS POSITIVE BEHAVIOR INCLUDING KINDNESS & CIVILITY |

## CLUBS CAN PRODUCE CUSTOM DIGITAL MAGAZINE & VIDEO PROGRAM RECOGNIZING MEMBER ACCOMPLISHMENTS

**REWARD**

| BUILDS CONFIDENCE, ACCOMPLISHMENTS, LONG-TERM RELATIONSHIPS & CAREER SKILLS | HELPS PROTECT AGAINST ANXIETY, LONELINESS, DEPRESSION, SUICIDE, ANTI-SOCIAL BEHAVIOR | CLUB & MEMBERS CAN BE FEATURED IN GLOBAL IPOP MAGAZINE & VIDEO PRODUCTIONS! |

# INTERNSHIP/MENTORSHIPS • REAL WORLD TRAINING
# MANAGEMENT & LEADERSHIP FOUNDATION SKILLS

**WHY OUR PROGRAMS ARE BETTER FOR YOUR CAREER DEVELOPMENT:** What truly makes our program different from other programs is that students work and learn on important real world programs where they get advanced skill training in their areas of interest and **the eight foundation disciplines** that everyone needs to move into management & leadership positions:

1. Communication
2. Business
3. Marketing
4. Management
5. Office Technology
6. Research
7. Problem Solving
8. Time Management

**COMPLETE YOUR PROGRAM & RECEIVE:**

1. Project Management (PMOROS) Course Certification
2. 8-Foundation Discipline Level 1 Course Certification
3. Custom Internship Completion Certificate
4. Career Opportunities / CPT - OPT - Sponsorship

**GRADUATE • UNDERGRADUATE • H.S. • INTERNATIONAL • CREDIT • CERTIFICATE • VOLUNTEER**

- Advertising
- Analytics
- Animation
- App Development
- Architecture / Interior Design
- Broadcasting
- Business
- Business Development
- Communication
- Computer Information Science
- Corporate Social Responsibility
- Data Analytics
- Design
- Economics
- Education
- Entrepreneurship
- Events
- Engineering
- Environment
- Financial Services
- Game Development
- Government
- Graphics
- Grant Writing
- Health
- Human Resources
- Insurance
- Information Tech.
- Journalism
- Legal Issues
- Leadership
- Management
- Marketing
- Merchandising
- Office Tech.
- Politics
- Programming
- Product Dev.
- Promotions
- Psychology
- Public Policy
- Public Relations
- Publishing
- Social Media
- SDGs
- Supply Chain Mgt
- Sustainability
- Taxation
- United Nations
- Video Production
- Visual Communication
- Web Development
- Wellness
- Writing
- Youth Initiatives

**BECOME PART OF OUR GROUND-BREAKING SOCIAL RESPONSIBILITY PROGRAMS WORKING ON GLOBAL COLLABORATIVE SYSTEMS ON AN INSTITUTIONAL LEVEL**

| HEALTH & WELL-BEING | EDUCATION & CAREER | EQUALITY/SOCIAL JUSTICE |
| --- | --- | --- |
| CIVILITY & KINDNESS | WORK/FAMILY BENEFITS | GLOBAL CITIZENSHIP |

OUR TRAINING PROGRAMS OPERATE ALL YEAR 'ROUND.

REGISTER ON OUR APP

GET PAK APP

**BOOKS**

**WEB & APPS**

**PROGRAMS**

**EVENTS**

# THE ESSENTIAL TRAINING EVERY STUDENT, EMPLOYEE & FAMILY NEEDS TO *WIN IN THE REAL WORLD

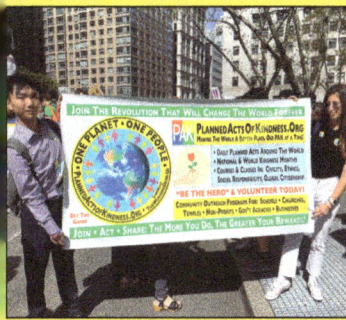

## INTERNSHIP/MENTORSHIP TRAINING:
### COMBINES EFFECTIVE PROVEN MULTI-DISCIPLINE SKILL TRAINING WITH REAL WORLD EXPERIENTIAL PROGRAMS

HELPS BRIDGE THE GAP BEEN CLASSROOM EDUCATION AND TASKED-BASED WORKER SKILLS TO OBJECTIVE-BASED ANALYTICAL TRAINING BASED ON THE PROPRIETARY PMOROS PROJECT MANAGEMENT SYSTEM DESIGNED TO BE PROACTIVE AND PROBLEM SOLVING MANAGEMENT AND LEADERSHIP TRAINING. RECOMMMENDED BY LEADING COLLEGES & UNIVERSITIES FOR UNDERGRADUATE & GRADUATE TRAINING IN OVER 50 DISCIPLINES.

## CAREER TRACK MANAGEMENT PROGRAM:
### 8-FOUNDATION SKILLS CERTIFICATION COURSES
### COMBINES ESSENTIAL DISCIPLINES & CRITICAL THINKING TO ENHANCE PERFORMANCE AT ALL LEVELS

NEED TO HAVE THESE 8-ESSENTIAL FOUNDATION SKILLS THAT EVERYONE IN EVERY FIELD HAS TO HAVE TO MOVE FROM WORKER MENTALITY INTO MANAGEMENT & LEADERSHIP

- COMMUNICATION
- BUSINESS
- MARKETING
- MANAGEMENT
- OFFICE SOFTWARE
- RESEARCH
- PROBLEM SOLVING
- TIME MANAGEMENT

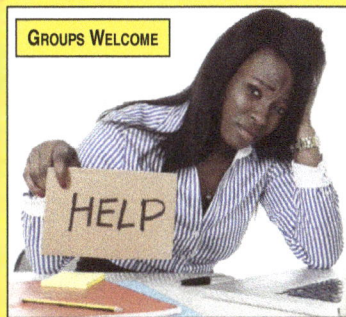

GROUPS WELCOME

HELP

## MANAGEMENT & LEADERSHIP TRAINING
### USING 8-FOUNDATION DISCIPLINES ON REAL WORLD PROGRAMS

WHETHER YOU ARE ...
- AN ENTREPRENEUR
- A BUSINESS OWNER
- IN A LEADERSHIP ROLE
- IN MANAGEMENT
- IN THE WORK FORCE
- IN SCHOOL

THIS TRAINING IS FOR YOU

WE HELP YOU BETTER UNDERSTAND AND ACHIEVE COMPANY, ORGANIZATIONAL AND CLIENT OBJECTIVES. HOW TO PROPERLY **RESEARCH, ANALYZE & SYNTHE-SIZE** INFORMATION UTILIZING CRITICAL THINKING.

HOW TO PROPERLY DO **PROJECT MANAGEMENT** AND **PROBLEM SOLVING** USING **COMMUNICATION, TIME MANAGEMENT** & OTHER **BUSINESS** RELATED SKILLS.

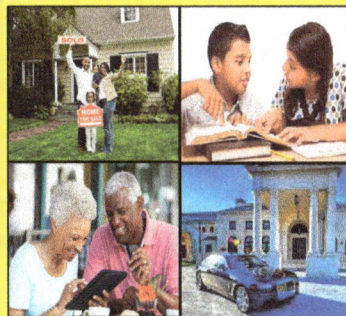

## MONEY MATTERS MASTERY: FINANCIAL LITERACY & PLANNING PROGAM

**COURSE OBJECTIVES:** (1) TO HELP YOU ANSWER YOUR FINANCIAL "WHY, HOW & WHAT" (2) TO UNDERSTAND HOW MONEY REALLY WORKS AND THE IMPORTANCE OF SECURING YOUR FINANCIAL FOUNDATION SO YOU CAN PROSPER AND GROW (3) TO WEATHER LIFE'S DIFFICULTIES THAT ARE SURE TO COME (CHRONIC, LONG TERM CARE, EMERGENCIES, TAXES, INFLATION, ETC.)

1ST. WHY ARE YOU WORKING? WHO & WHAT'S IT FOR?
2ND. HOW DOES MONEY REALLY WORK & HOW CAN IT WORK FOR ME?
3RD. WHAT'S YOUR PLAN? IS IT SAFE? CAN IT GROW, PROTECT & SAVE YOU MONEY?

"MEASURE OF PERSON'S WEALTH, NOT HOW MUCH THEY MAKE, BUT HOW MUCH THEY KEEP"

# OUR PROGRAMS CAN MAKE ALL THE DIFFERENCE. TAKE ACTION: ASK TO PROVIDE

*BRING THIS TO SCHOOL/WORK ASK THEM TO CONTACT US (57)

# ATHLETES: H.S., COLLEGE, PRO · THE KEYS TO SUCCESS
## EVERY STUDENT, PARENT, TEACHER & ADMINISTRATOR SHOULD DEMAND

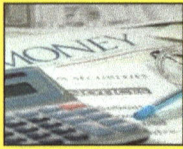

1. FINANCIAL LITERACY & PLANNING FOR ENTIRE FAMILY
2. CAREER TRACK MANAGEMENT 8 FOUNDATION DISCIPLINE CERTIFICATION
3. INTERNSHIP/MENTORSHIP PROGRAMS BASED ON CAREER
4. REAL WORLD COLLABORATION PROGRAMS FOR GLOBAL QUALITY OF LIFE

# ODDS FOR GOING PRO IN THE NFL

**300K KIDS** — seniors play high school football annually with the hope of getting a college scholarship

**COLLEGE 70K** — college athletes in the NCAA are all striving to reach the NFL

**300 MAKING IT** — athletes make it to an NFL roster yearly out of the 70,000 players from high school

**LIFETIME 150** — of the 300 athletes that made it to the NFL will have a career lasting more than 3 years

OF THE 7,200,000 HIGH SCHOOL STUDENTS ATHLETES, APPROXIMATELY 6% OR 430,000 EVER MAKE THE CUT TO PARTICIPATE AT THE NCAA LEVEL IN COLLEGE.

HIGH SCHOOL TO DIVISION I IS SIGNIFICANTLY MORE DIFFICULT:

| MEN: | H.S. PARTICIPANTS | NCAA | HS% TO NCAA | HS% TO DIV. I | D.I. PART. |
|---|---|---|---|---|---|
| FOOTBALL: | 1,006,013 | 73,712 | 7.30% | 2.90% | 29,174 |
| BASKETBALL: | 540,769 | 18,816 | 3.50% | 1.00% | 5,408 |
| BASEBALL: | 482,740 | 36,011 | 7.50% | 2.20% | 10,620 |

ASK YOUR SCHOOL OR YOUR EMPLOYER IF THEY PROVIDE THESE PAK & ONE PLANET ONE PEOPLE PROGRAMS
58 ADD OUR PROGRAMS & SHOW HOW MUCH YOU CARE FOR YOUR PEOPLE

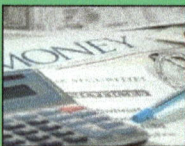

# MONEY MATTERS MASTERY
## FINANCIAL LITERACY & PLANNING COURSE

# WHAT'S YOUR WHY?

**1st. Know your Why. Why are you working? Who's it for? What's it for?**

**CHILDREN?**

**HOME OWNERSHIP?**

**RETIREMENT?**

**WEALTH?**

**2nd. Know Your Hows.** How does money work & can it work for me? Not based on what Wall Street/Banks say. They have their own agenda. It's not yours. How much will I really need?

**3rd. What's Your Plan?** You have to have a plan that's safe, can grow, protects your assets & reduces your taxes. Unfortunately, it's not your company's benefits plan.

**Course Objectives:** To help you answer your financial "Why, How & What"; to understand how money really works & the importance of securing your Financial Foundation so you can prosper & grow & weather life's difficulties that are sure to come.

Income 529 401k Stocks Pensions 403b Taxes Creditors Bonds Penalties Judgements Investments Custom Quality Compound 1035 Retirement Financial College Safety Family 7702 Bankruptcy Social Insurance Rollovers Expenses Annuities Careers 457 College Mortgage Wealth Income Rule IRA Debt Wealth Growth

## S SAFETY?
GUARANTEED FLOOR: MONEY IS NOT SUBJECT TO MARKET LOSS

## G GROWTH?
COMPOUND INTEREST: INTEREST EARNED ANNUALLY ADDED TO PRINCIPAL

### WHAT DO YOU HAVE IN YOUR FOUNDATION?

## P PROTECTION?
INSURANCE: PAYS CASH DUE TO CHRONIC ILLNESS OR DEATH OR USE FOR RETIREMT

## T TAX FREE?
PAY NO TAXES: 100% TAX & PENALTY-FREE CASH ACCUMULATION/DISTRIB.

## MONEY MATTERS MASTERY CLASS OUTLINE
Six Video Classes, Workbook Assignments & Zoom

### Class 1: Introduction & Overview
— Your Why of Why's
— How People Allocate Their Money
— The Big Zero

### Class 2: Debt
— Debt Management Strategies
— Protecting Your "Why"
— The DIME Method
— The Importance of Paying Yourself First

— The Time Value Relationship of Money

### Class 3: Savings & Growth
— Five Factors for Building Wealth
— The Four Blocks to Building Your Financial Foundation

### Class 4: Insurance: "The Big Three"
Risk Mgmt & Asset Protection
— Life Insurance Programs
— IRA vs. IUL, 1035 Explained

### Class 5: Taxation
— The X-Curve
— Tax Now. Tax Later. Tax Never?
— The Rule of 72
— IRC 7702 Tax Advantages

### Class 6: Benefit Plan Illustration & Career Track Planning
— Custom Benefit Plans
— The Cashflow Quadrant
— Advanced Financial Services
— Supplemental Services

# FINANCIAL LITERACY & PLANNING
## TWD • MONEY MATTERS MASTERY • CUSTOM BENEFITS PROGRAMS

## INDIVIDUALS & FAMILIES ARE IN A FINANCIAL CRISIS:

*71% of all Americans don't believe they will be able to fully retire*
*The average family has over $10,000 in credit card debt*
*50% of your annual retirement income may go to the govt as taxes increase*
*7 out of 10 people will need Long Term Care & Can't Afford to Pay for It*

## "THE WORKING DEAD" IS AVAILABLE FOR INDIVIDUALS & ORGANIZATIONS
## IT CAN BE BRANDED TO EXCEED CSR OBJECTIVES OR FUND-RAISING GOALS

THE WORKING DEAD

LYLE BENJAMIN

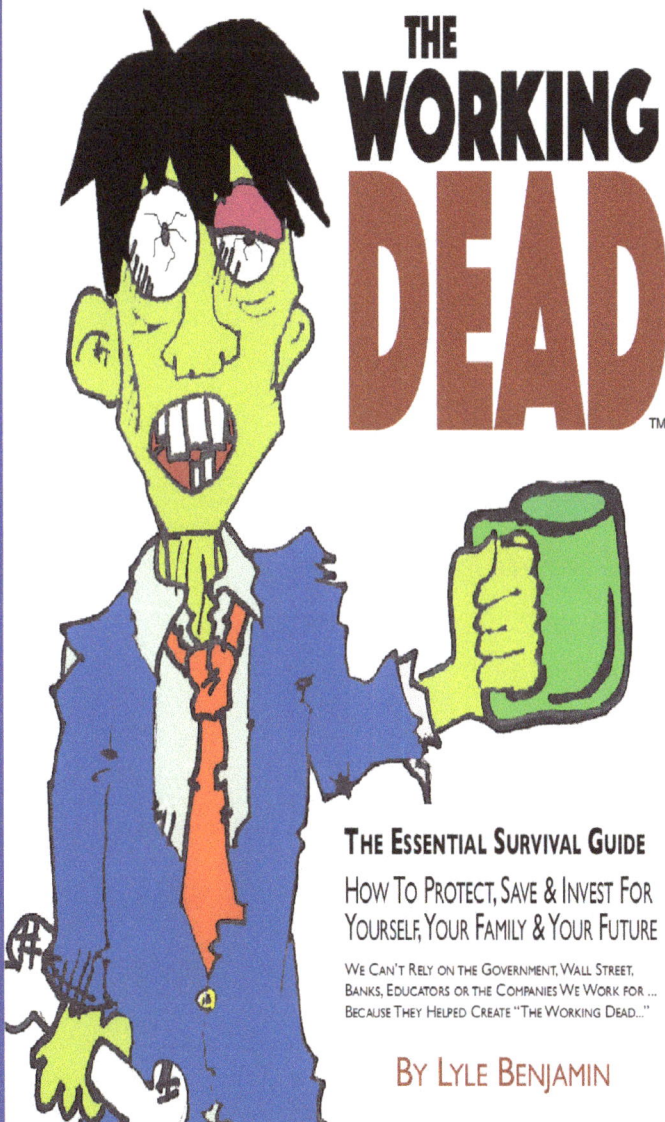

16T
PRESS

# THE WORKING DEAD™

### THE ESSENTIAL SURVIVAL GUIDE

HOW TO PROTECT, SAVE & INVEST FOR
YOURSELF, YOUR FAMILY & YOUR FUTURE

WE CAN'T RELY ON THE GOVERNMENT, WALL STREET,
BANKS, EDUCATORS OR THE COMPANIES WE WORK FOR ...
BECAUSE THEY HELPED CREATE "THE WORKING DEAD..."

## BY LYLE BENJAMIN

**Mission:**
To help people understand and build a
solid financial foundation that benefits
themselves and their families not wall
street, banks, companies and the gov't.

**Issues & Solutions:**
Regardless of your education,
income or success, most people:
• Don't understand how money works
• Earn a low rate of return on money
• Spend too much of their monthly income
• Are drowning in debt
• Pay too much in taxes
• Have little money for emergencies
• Won't meet their retirement goals
• Won't be able to fund children's college
• Don't have proper insurance protection
• Don't have Chronic Care or LTC protection
• Will have to work after they should retire
• Will fail to leave a positive financial legacy
• Will fail to achieve the "Quality of Life"
  they desire

**Take Action:**
Get All The Tools You Need To Properly:

• Build for Retirement while Protecting
  against devastation of Long-Term Care
  401K, 403B, 457 plans are not the answer

• Build Wealth Safely with Tax-Free, Penalty-
  Free withdrawals at any age thru IR Code
  Stocks are not the answer

• Reduce Effects of Inflation, Low Interest
  Banks are not the answer

• Fund Your Children's College Education
  529 plans are not the answer

61

"RECONSIDER YOUR DEFINITIONS. WE ARE PRONE TO JUDGE SUCCESS BY THE INDEX OF OUR SALARIES OR THE SIZE OF OUR AUTOMOBILES RATHER THAN BY THE QUALITY OF OUR SERVICE AND RELATIONSHIP TO MANKIND."
— DR. MARTIN LUTHER KING, JR

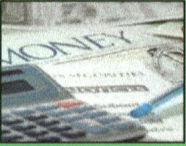

# FINANCIAL QUALITY OF LIFE
## INCREASING INCOME ◼ INCREASING BENEFITS

# IT'S NOT HOW MUCH MONEY YOU MAKE. IT'S HOW MUCH YOU GET TO KEEP. PERIOD.

## WHICH WAY DO YOU EARN YOUR MONEY?
### LEARN TO DO WHAT RICH DO & BE ON RIGHT SIDE: B & I

## WHAT DO YOU HAVE IN YOUR FOUNDATION?
### DON'T HAVE ALL FOUR? TIME FOR A NEW PLAN

### E
**EMPLOYEE**
WORKS TO MAKE OTHERS RICH. NO WORK NO PAY 90% OF POPULATION

### B
**BIG BUSINESS**
TRADES MONEY FOR TIME EARNS PASSIVE INCOME FROM OTHERS WORKING

### S
**SAFETY?**
GUARANTEED FLOOR: MONEY IS NOT SUBJECT TO MARKET LOSS

### G
**GROWTH?**
COMPOUND INTEREST: INTEREST EARNED ANNUALLY ADDED TO PRINCIPAL

**HAVE MONEY WORK FOR YOU, EVEN WHEN YOU'RE NOT WORKING**

**401K, 403B, 457 PLANS GIVE ONLY OPPORTUNITY FOR G**

### S
**SMALL BIZ OWNER**
TIRED OF LACK OF CONTROL STILL EMPLOYEE OF OWN BIZ

### I
**INVESTMENT INCOME**
PORTION OF EARNINGS GROWTH FOR FUTURE

### P
**PROTECTION?**
INSURANCE: PAYS CASH DUE TO CHRONIC ILLNESS OR DEATH OR USE FOR RETIREMT

### T
**TAX FREE?**
PAY NO TAXES: 100% TAX & PENALTY-FREE CASH ACCUMULATION/DISTRIB.

## WE HAVE THE THREE SOLUTIONS YOU NEED: EDUCATION, OPPORTUNITY & AFFORDABILITY

**FROM BOOKS, WORKSHOPS, COURSES COVERING FINANCIAL CONCEPTS & PLANNING NOT TAUGHT IN COLLEGES EVEN IF FINANCE, ECON, BUSINESS MAJOR**

**FREE FINANCIAL NEEDS ANALYSIS & PLANNING RECOMMENDATIONS**

**SUPPLEMENTAL & FULL-TIME INCOME PROGRAMS WHERE YOU GET TO BE THE HERO BY HELPING OTHERS**

**MEDICAL   EDUCATORS   VETERANS**

**YOU SPEND YOUR LIFE PROTECTING & HELPING. NOW IT'S TIME FOR YOU & YOUR FAMILY.**

### ESSENTIALS YOU NEED TO KNOW:
- Properly Build for Retirement. 401k, 403b, 457 plans are NOT the answer.
- Fund Children's College Education. 529 plans are NOT the answer.
- Reduce the Effects of Inflation on Your Money. Banks are NOT the answer.
- Build Wealth Tax-Free by IRS Code. Stocks & IRAs are NOT the answer.
- How to Get Long Term & Chronic Care. No Add'l Spending or Bankruptcy.
- How the Government Can Help Pay for Your Retirement. Not Pension or S.S.

**64**  CAREER, SERVICE, LEADERSHIP, INCOME THRU OUR ORGS

**EDUCATION, CAREER TRAINING, INCOME & CUSTOM BENEFITS PROGRAMS ARE AVAILABLE DIRECTLY FROM US BUT PLEASE ASK YOUR ORG OR EMPLOYER TO ADD TO HELP OTHERS**

# CUSTOM BENEFIT PLANS
## NEW OR SUPPLEMENTAL PROGRAMS FOR INDIVIDUALS & ORGS OF ANY SIZE

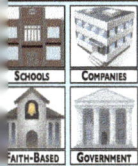

# COMPANY VOLUNTEERS FOR QL

**Q: WHAT'S YOUR ORG'S COMMITMENT TO BETTERING YOUR EMPLOYEES? YOUR COMMUNITY & YOUR COMPANY?**

**A: HAVING YOUR EMPLOYEES VOLUNTEER WITH PAK's/IPOP's SOCIAL RESPONSIBILITY PROGRAMS & YOUR ORGANIZATION GETTING THE CREDIT**

## ALL FIELDS • ALL DISCIPLINES • ALL COUNTRIES • ALL WELCOME

BUSINESS • COMMUNICATIONS • FUND-RAISING • HR • ENGINEERING • PROJECT MGT • PUBLISHING • SOCIAL MEDIA • SUSTAINABILITY

**BE THE HERO: HELP SUPPORT INITIATIVES that MAKE A TREMENDOUS DIFFERENCE to INDIVIDUALS, FAMILIES, COMMUNITIES, YOUR CLIENTS & YOUR COMPANY**

## LOCAL, NATIONAL, GLOBAL ENGAGEMENT PROGRAMS

### BUILD, MANAGE, LEAD A TEAM!

**Programs & Initiatives**
- Collaboration Think Tank Professional Volunteer
- The Karma Club Global Ambassador
- E-Quality Education (E-QL): Quality of Life thru PAK
- One Planet One People (IPOP) Clubs
- Club Magazine/Video Program Mentor
- Internships/Mentorships: Real World Training
- Career Track Management 8-Foundation Certification Courses
- Money Matters Mastery: Financial Literacy & Planning Course
- "The Working Dead" Financial Literacy Book Sponsorship
- Basketball & Bonding: Parent & Child Legacy Building Clinics

**Work/Life Balance & Quality of Life**
- Financial Quality of Life: Increasing Income, Increasing Benefits
- Custom Benefit Plans: New/Supplemental for Individuals/Orgs
- Project KOPE: Help, Happiness & Wellness thru Kindness
- The Dirty Dozen: Team Building to the Next Level
- One Planet One People: Home/Office Workspace QL Hubs
- Rooftop/Building Sustainability Solutions: Bringing Indoors Out
- One Green World EduMarket

**Cause Driven Books, Programs, Initiatives, Events**
- 16 Things Cause Driven Books: Education/Action/Workshops
- Do You Have a Cause to Promote? How to Partner
- SIREM: Social Institutional Reform/Equality Month. Video Series
- SIREM Speaks! People Providing Solutions. Video Series
- Legacy Lifelines Memorial: Creating Legacies for Lost Loved Ones

**Causes & Campaigns**
- One Planet One People One Table One World
- The Smile & Wave (S.A.W.) Challenge: Create Smile Chains
- Barter "Bucket List" Fund-Raising Challenge
- The Great Pizza Peace Plan Challenge: PAK Kindness Pledge
- The ONE Challenge: Raise $1 for Every One Person fm Billionaires
- Crazy Ambitious Activities Program (CAAP) Ultimate Volunteering
- The Global Campaign for Kindness: Creating PSAs
- Donation, Partnership & Sponsorship Outreach Campaigns

**Got More Time?**
- 2022-25 One Planet One People (IPOP) Summits
- IPOP The Game: The Fight for Survival of the Human Race
- IPOP Portal: Connecting People to Collaborative Global Systems
- Community Partnership Centers

**NO MATTER WHAT YOUR SIZE, YOUR ORG'S HR/CSR MISSION SHOULD INCLUDE VOLUNTEERING**

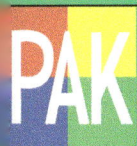

**PAK**

**ANXIOUS?**
**STRESSED?**
**LONELY?**
**DEPRESSED?**

**We're Here to Help.**

**Youth & Adult Health & Wellness thru Kindness**

### Project KOPE

**PLANNEDACTS.ORG**
PLANNED ACTS OF KINDNESS
WORKING FOR THE BETTERMENT OF KIDS,
PEOPLE & THE PLANET!

**Scan the QR Code & Visit Project KOPE**
Schools • Non-Profits • Governments • Businesses

**"TO CREATE A STATE OF HAPPINESS TAKES NO LONGER THAN TO ENGAGE IN DOING A GOOD DEED ..." – CATHERINE PULSIFER**

### HEALTH, HAPPINESS & WELLNESS PROGRAM

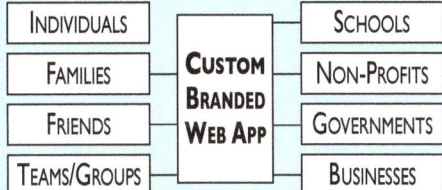

| INDIVIDUALS | | SCHOOLS |
|---|---|---|
| FAMILIES | **CUSTOM BRANDED WEB APP** | NON-PROFITS |
| FRIENDS | | GOVERNMENTS |
| TEAMS/GROUPS | | BUSINESSES |

**RECOGNITION/REWARDS • TEAM BUILDING**

### GETTING STARTED STEPS:

1. SCAN QR CODE & SAVE APP
2. GO TO PROJECT KOPE, NAV MENU
3. CHOOSE YOUR PLAN
4. TAKE 1ST QUALITY OF LIFE SURVEY
5. DO YOUR MONTHLY ACHIEVEMENTS
6. RECEIVE RECOGNITION, REWARDS
7. RETAKE SURVEYS
8. GREATER HEALTH, HAPPINESS IN YOU & OTHERS

67

# TEAM BUILDING TO THE NEXT LEVEL

## WHEN THE MISSION MATTERS, IT'S TIME TO STEP UP & ANSWER THE CALL
## ASSEMBLE YOUR TEAM & PACK UP & MOVE OUT. THE FATE OF THE WORLD IS IN YOUR HANDS

Use PAK App

# Do You Have What It Takes ... To Be A Member of The Dirty Dozen 2?

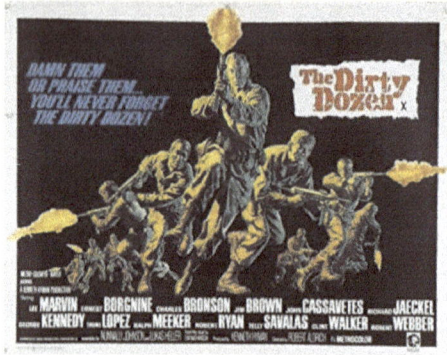

**WHO:** Top People of Influence

**WHAT:** Working to Change the World

**WHERE:** Here. Act Nationally, Impact Globally

**WHY:** To Right Wrongs & Create Quality of Life for All

**WHEN:** Starting Now, Over a 90-Day Period

**HOW:** Review PLANNED ACTS OF KINDNESS' ACTION PROGRAMS Aligned with all 17 United Nations SDGs

Choose Your Outreach & Engagement Programs

Work with Other Members of Your Dirty Dozen Team

Engage & Inspire Millions of People: From the Grassroots Up to The Top Down

**COMMITMENT:** Check in Minimum of Twice Weekly for Tactical Briefings & Progress Reports

**GOALS & LEVELS:** What's Your Dirty Dozen Team Engagement Goal & Success at the End of Your 90-Day Cycle?
Friend: 1,000/5,000/10,000; Activist: 10,000/50,000/100,000; Altruist: 100,000/500,000/1,000,000
Humanitarian: 1,000,000/5,000,000, 10,000,000; Philanthropist: 10,000,000;50,000,000/100,000,000

**REQUIREMENTS:** All Members of the Dirty Dozen Pledge Not to Shave (somewhere) for 90 Days During Their Mission

**START-UP TACTICAL KIT:** Customized Dirty Dozen Team Poster
PAK Pin & QLA (Quality of Life for All) Pin
Karma Coins
Planned Acts Wristbands
One Planet One People Stickers
Customized Digital Team Cards
Customized Team App & Web Pages (optional)

**Create Your Own Dirty Dozen Team**

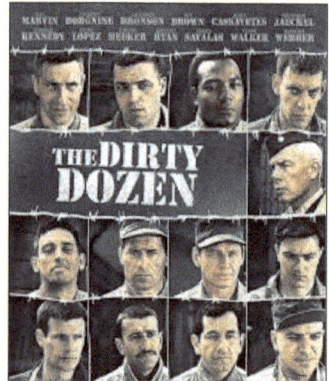

**MISSION READY:** Your 90-Day Mission Begins When Team Assembled
Name Your DIRTY DOZEN Team
Make Your Custom Dirty Dozen Team Poster
Pledge a Donation to the Cause
Enlist Others to Join Your Team
Film & Document Your Progress Along the Way

**RECRUITS:** Engage In Your Mission
Recruit Others & Expand Your Dirty Dozen Team

**REWARDS:** Personalized Shaving Kit
Certificate for Outstanding Service (level obtained)
WAM! (Words & Actions Matter!) Mug
Signed Dirty Dozen Team Poster
Dirty Dozen Team Movie

PLANNED ACTS
OF KINDNESS
presents
A "ONE PLANET - ONE PEOPLE"
PRODUCTION

screenplay by LYLE BENJAMIN, FOUNDER • produced by PLANNED ACTS OF KINDNESS • directed by UN SDGs • PLANNEDACTS.ORG/dozen
help@plannedacts.org • 212.213.0257 • planned acts of kindness is a 501(c)3 non-profit organization working for the betterment of kids, people & the planet

# WORK/LIFE BALANCE: QUALITY OF LIFE

## Threshold Architects & Sustainability Partners

### Work/Life Balance Hubs

As an architect that has worked with top companies around the world, I was afforded the opportunity to integrate my visions into company designs. Being environmentally conscious was always something I, and my team, incorporated into our builds.

When the opportunity arose for me to partner with founder Lyle Benjamin and actively collaborate on bringing my design, environmental and sustainability knowledge together with work/life balance programs of Planned Acts and One Planet One People — I literally jumped ship.

Here was my chance to make a huge impact on people's Quality of Life that far outstripped anything I've ever done before — my work with Apple, Microsoft, Sony CIGNA, Deloitte, McKinsey, General Electric, Procter & Gamble, Gucci, Tiffany's, Calvin Klein, etc. notwithstanding.

### Quality of Life

Not only did we create the four types of Work/Life Balance Hubs — Global, National, Community & Neighborhood — but we stocked them full of Quality of Life programs and initiatives designed to value employees, contractors and their families while setting the standard for Corporate Social Responsibility.

Whether you work within a small organization, a large non-profit or a multinational there are HR-related programs that can help with recruitment and retainment of personnel: Programs on financial literacy and planning; no company cost supplemental custom benefits programs; health, happiness & wellness programs; career track management programs for skill and leadership development; and team building and volunteer programs that can garner tremendous positive public relations.

If these weren't enough incentives for companies to jump on-board, this aspect is the clincher — many of the programs are customizable to meet shareholder and stakeholder objectives! Wow.

### One Green World EduMarket

But our collaboration doesn't end here. This is only the beginning. The next phase is the launch of our One Green World EduMarket. OGW is designed to offer people and institutions (think of Planned Acts of Kindness' 5 x 5 audience) a guide to products, goods and services that have a positive impact on people and the planet's Quality of Life.

The objective is to provide actionable (mostly environmental) solutions that can be implemented by people, companies, and governments all over the world with the goal of having cumulative benefits in addressing the problems.

Many of the items offered will be provided from the research and solutions of the Collaboration Think Tank Teams. It's important to note the solutions come primarily from three sources: Scientific, business, and academic in much the same way as PAK's Collaboration Think Tank Teams are constructed.

### The Next Step — It's All About You.

You don't have to be the CEO in your organization to take this to take advantage of these programs. These programs are created for your benefit as well as your company's. Just take this to HR and share. And if your company doesn't have a dedicated HR department, then share it with the owners. It's to their benefit as well as yours. (See the following pages for more information.)

Whether people want to explore our work or set up a consultation, it all goes through the PAK app. There you can get links to brochures, score some checklists to help you deal with processes, set up a consultation to discuss your objectives and even add your product, goods or services to the One Planet Green EduMart.

We are all in this together, and only by working together through programs that provide Quality of Life can we really obtain Quality of Life.

**For myself, and my team, we look forward to being a small part of the success of the One Planet One People movement**

# ONE PLANET ONE PEOPLE HOME/OFFICE WORKSPACE QUALITY OF LIFE HUBS

**Threshold Architects & Sustainability Partners:** Where Company Culture & Corporate Social Responsibility are Designed into Every Environment

## We Must Adapt to Survive

The simple but powerful concept behind One Planet One People is that we must stop the fractional approach to solving global issues and collaborate to succeed. And what does success mean? It means Quality of Life for people around the world: Access to affordable food, health care, education, quality employment at living wages, respect for all races, religions, genders — all on a planet that isn't trying to eradicate us as if we were a virus damaging its ecosystem.

## The Effect of COVID-19 on the Office

Regarding traditional office space, the big take-away we learned from COVID-19 was that office workers no longer had to work in centralized locations to do their jobs. That didn't meant that companies didn't want their workers to come back to the office once it was deemed safe to do so. On the other hand, as we are now seeing, many workers are not happy with going back to the same old same old. They want something different. Staying at home 24/7 isn't the answer, but going back to their office doesn't sit well also.

## The Increasing Importance of Work/Life Balance

COVID-19 showed us how dramatically and profoundly our lives can change due to external circumstances beyond our control. And by COVID taking away our ability to be with our families and friends, how important those relationships are to our overall happiness and well-being. By witnessing others suffer in similar and worse circumstances over such an extended time, in essence, it gave us a lesson in prioritizing humanity over work.

## The Role of Corporate Social Responsibility

Whether rightly or wrongly, it seemed to some that CSR was just another way corporations rolled out marketing buzz words to capture people's attention with little being done on the substantive end that benefited something other than the bottom line. But over time as customer and employee became more knowledgeable, they also became more demanding that companies lived up to their own "do good" claims. And many companies have changed to do just that especially in the areas of carbon footprints, safety standards, gender sensitivity training.

70

(con't)

**DESIRED SENSIBILITIES FOR SPACE**

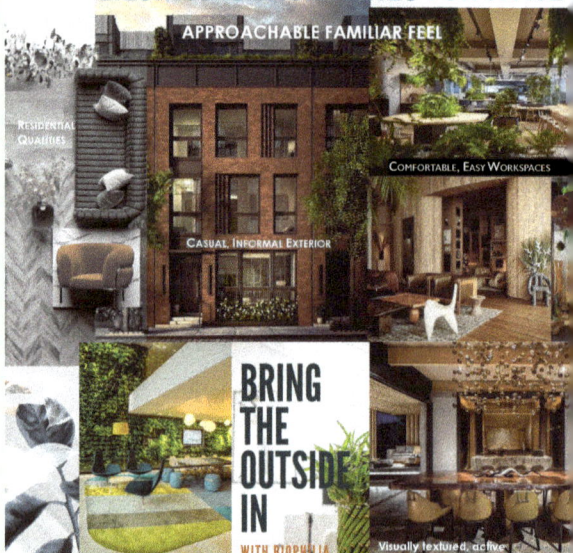

APPROACHABLE FAMILIAR FEEL

RESIDENTIAL QUALITIES

COMFORTABLE, EASY WORKSPACES

CASUAL, INFORMAL EXTERIOR

BRING THE OUTSIDE IN WITH BIOPHILIA

Visually textured, active

## Long-Term Solutions

**Rethinking floor plans**

We can also rethink floor plans to provide room for people to "breathe" in a more hygienic environment. While many companies are considering ways to de-densify their offices in the short term, there are more permanent ways to achieve this goal by altering building forms.

Ultimately, one thing we've learned from the isolation we've experienced as a result of the pandemic is the degree to which humans are social animals. We value human connection, and we'd like to rejoin our colleagues again — The lessons we learn from this experience help us design environments that promote health and wellness as values that are integrated in our design. (con't)

PAK Founder, Lyle Benjamin has partnered with award-winning environmental **architect Alice Mok** to create **One Planet One People** Home/Office Workspace Quality of Life Hubs – Hubs provide employees with opportunities to work in smaller hybrid home/office environments with shorter commutes and added quality of life benefits packages.

Hubs are fully customizable spaces that exceed both company office and employee objectives for productivity, sustainability, environmental factors, technology, connectivity, comfort, safety, and style while adding in additional programs for management & leadership training, team building, corporate social responsibility, global citizenship, volunteerism, community engagement, health & wellness, and supplemental custom benefits for employees, contractors, and their families.

## Companies Are Facing a Big Problem

While these efforts are laudable, they don't go far enough, wide enough, deep enough or fast enough, especially concerning one of the company's most valuable assets is its people. For many, many, many companies — whether small, medium and large — their people are not waking up looking forward to going to work, and that's a big problem.

## The Solution Is Simple

C-Suiters must treat your employees like you are treated — with respect, kindness, support, opportunity, and an architecturally designed work environment that imbues positive energy. In short, provide them with Quality of Life that acts as part of the foundation that extends from their work into their personal life.

## Implementation Is Simple

Companies collaborate with PAK and One Planet One People to provide access to a variety of CSR, team building, volunteer, and employee and family benefit programs for employees, contractors, spouses, and children. Home/Office Hubs can also be configured to meet the needs of any size team, group, department, division, or company in any location setting or building structure.

## Combining Comfort, Function & Responsibility

For many employees the questions that still need to be addressed in the short and medium-term are: Where will I work? How safe will I be? Under what conditions will I work? Is it really necessary for me to commute all that way? Can't I work more locally with my team? Is this work situation right for me? It is good for my health and well-being? Is it good for my family? For my future?

Threshold Architects SP and One Planet One People have the collaboration solutions to these questions that help provide the foundation for building Quality of Life. And together we can design and build a better world for everyone.

Contact Alice for more on partnering Threshold/1POP: 212.213.0257

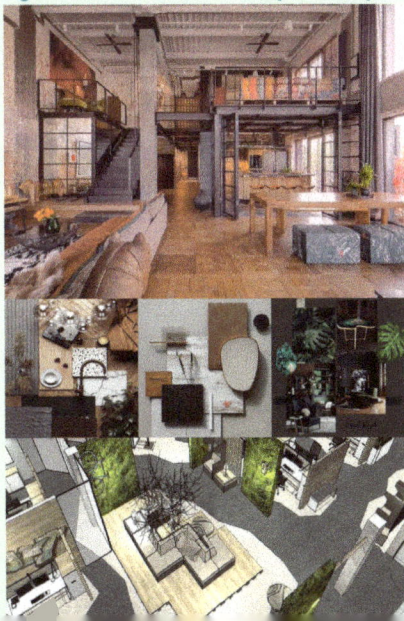

## One Planet One People Quality of Life Programs

> **Career Track Management:** PMOROS Project Management System, 8-Foundation Skills Certification Courses with Team Training Practical Modules

> **Team Building Programs:** Great Pizza Peace Plan Challenge, Collaboration Think Tank, CAAP, One Table One World, The SAW Campaign, The Dirty Dozen,

> **Personal, Family & Financial Development:** The Karma Club — "Making the World a Better Place One PAK at a Time," Basketball & Bonding — Parent & Child Program, Project KOPE — "Your Guide to Greater Health, Happiness & Wellness through Planned Acts of Kindness"

> **Volunteer Programs** — SIREM, E-QL, 1POP CLUBS, Money Matters Mastery Financial Literacy & Planning Course/Program, Custom Benefits Program

71

# IF YOU'VE GOT A ROOF OVER YOUR HEAD
## ISN'T IT TIME TO LEARN HOW REWARDING

### TELL US YOUR PROBLEMS
- Climate Change
- Sustainability
- Air, Water, Noise Pollution
- Urban Heat Island Effect
- Energy Consumption
- Water Waste Management
- Space Management

BRINGING THE INDOORS OUT & THE OUTDOORS TO THE SKY

planet.
innovations

72 SDGs 9 & 11

Health & Wellness

An Urban Oasis

Team Collaborations

Event Space

# YOU MAY BE PART OF THE PROBLEM.
## IT CAN BE TO BE PART OF THE SOLUTION?

### WE'LL PROVIDE THE SOLUTIONS

- Creating a Zero Carbon Emissions Building
- Highest & Best Use of Materials & Technology
- Reducing Energy Consumption, Adding Protection
- Safeguarding Water Resources by Maximizing Reuse & Minimizing Consumption
- Creating Resilient, Flexible Structures, Adding Value
- Maximizing All Stages of the Building's Lifecycle

Gaming Zone

### CSR SOLUTIONS FOR YOUR COMPANY & YOUR PEOPLE:

- Creating External Green Environments
- Promoting Health & Well-Being
- Greater Productivity
- Increased Creativity
- Greater Retention
- Reduced Overhead
- Connecting People & Communities

Meetings

Coffee Bar & Lounge

Worktables

ଔ ଔ ଔ

Threshold Architects & Sustainability Partners
(pages 69-73 on PAK App)

# ONE GREEN WORLD EduMart

## ENSURING QUALITY OF LIFE THRU SUSTAINABLE & RESPONSIBLE PRODUCTS

# WE ARE AT THE TIPPING POINT FOR QUALITY OF LIFE FOR BILLIONS

  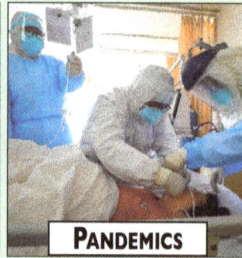 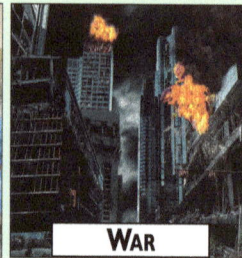

**CLIMATE CHANGE** | **POLLUTION** | **PANDEMICS** | **WAR**

# WHATEVER REPORTS YOU HEAR FROM THE EXPERTS, THINGS ARE MUCH WORSE & WE AREN'T SCARED ENOUGH AS INDIVIDUALS & INSTITUTIONS: WE NEED TO DO MORE.

# WORKING WITH IPOP's COLLABORATION THINK TANK ONE GREEN WORLD EduMARKET IS THE INNOVATIVE HUB FOR GREEN PRODUCTS, GOODS & SERVICES

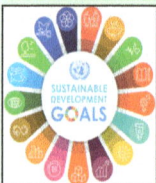     

**CONSUMPTION** | **LIFESTYLE** | **HOME** | **OFFICE** | **BUILDINGS** | **CONSTRUCTION**

# USERS/PROVIDERS SIGN-UP TODAY FOR PRE-LAUNCH SPECIALS

   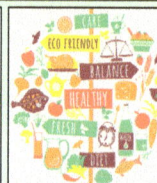  

**74** MANUFACTURE | **FOOD** | **ENERGY** | **HEALTH** | **SERVICES** | **COMMUNITY**

# SECTION VII:
# CAUSE-DRIVEN BOOKS, PROGRAMS, INITIATIVES & EVENTS

"You have to be burning with an idea, or a problem, or a wrong that you want to right. If you're not passionate enough from the start, you'll never stick it out."
— Steve Jobs

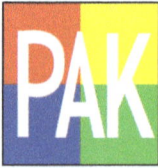

# Do You Have a Cause to Promote?
## How To Partner on a 16 Things Book/Workshop/App

| Your Why | Our Why |
|---|---|
| You want to cut through media clutter & make a lasting impact on your audience that inspires them to take action on your cause | Our mission is to partner with organizations, businesses & governments to provide collaborative & scalable education & action programs that promote Quality of Life |

**The How & The What**

- Fully Customized Book Tailored to Your Cause
- Book Foreward Written by Your CEO
- 4C Promotional Pages

- Your CEO's Name on Front Book Cover
- Full Chapter on Your Organization's Mission
- Workshops, Website & Branded App Tie-Ins

| 1 Choose Your Book Subject | 2 Get The Book Plan Material | 3 Finalize Your Book Plan | 4 Engage The *Featured Experts | 5 Promote On S.M. Networks | 6 Book Distribution |
|---|---|---|---|---|---|
| 1 NO POVERTY<br>2 ZERO HUNGER<br>3 GOOD HEALTH AND WELL-BEING<br>4 QUALITY EDUCATION<br>5 GENDER EQUALITY<br>6 CLEAN WATER AND SANITATION<br>7 AFFORDABLE AND CLEAN ENERGY<br>8 DECENT WORK AND ECONOMIC GROWTH<br>9 INDUSTRY INNOVATION AND INFRASTRUCTURE<br>10 REDUCED INEQUALITIES<br>11 SUSTAINABLE CITIES AND COMMUNITIES<br>12 RESPONSIBLE CONSUMPTION AND PRODUCTION<br>13 CLIMATE ACTION<br>14 LIFE BELOW WATER<br>15 LIFE ON LAND<br>16 PEACE AND JUSTICE STRONG INSTITUTIONS<br>17 PARTNERSHIPS FOR THE GOALS | Use the link to go to the book section at PlannedActs.Org<br><br>Choose the files to download<br><br>• Executive Summary<br>• Sample Media Kit<br>• Book Plan Options:<br>A. Sponsorship<br>B. Partnership<br>C. NPO Fund-Raiser<br>• Program Guide | A. Sponsorship:<br>Sponsor Funded Books<br>• 100,000 Book Run<br>• 35,000 Sponsor Copies<br>• May Include SIREM, Project KOPE, Clubs<br>B. Partnership: Featured Expert Funded Books<br>• 32 Experts per Book<br>• 10,000 Minimum Book Order<br>C. Non-Profit Fund-Raiser:<br>• No Minimum Required | Your organization provides a Featured Expert contact spreadsheet for your book or Planned Acts develops it from Industry Experts & People of Influence in the respective field(s)<br><br>Planned Acts Provides Invitation Materials & Performs Book Interviews:<br>• Sample Phone Script<br>• Email Letter Content<br>• Interview Questions<br>• Video Interview (30-Min) | Before the book is printed we'll help you develop campaigns to impress share holders & stakeholders<br><br>Social Media Messages & Graphics for Facebook, Instagram, Linked-In, Twitter as well as Videos for Youtube and TikTok<br><br>Produce & post consistent quality content on your networks & with influencers to get quantifiable results | When the book is printed, in addition to traditional areas of book distribution, we'll inspire people to take action from the grassroots up with individuals — to the top down engaging institutions — schools, faith-based orgs, npo's, governments & businesses — all to get people informed, educated, engaged, educated & inspired to take action on a local, national & global scale on your cause |

| 7 Increased Branding | 8 Increased Marketing | 9 Increased Media & Publicity | 10 Increased Philanthropy | 11 Increased Revenue |
|---|---|---|---|---|

## Partnership: Featured Expert Funded Book Example

**PAK**

### Our NPO's Mission Is To Help Your Org Grow. Your Book Turns Members Into Celebrity Rock Stars!

**$25,000**
Minimum Revenue for Organization

**$300,000**
Free Branding Package

**32 Org Leaders**
Speak Out On 16 Important Issues
people face in their lives and what needs to be done to help solve these problems.

**Featuring:**
- Important Issues/Solutions
- Color Headshot
- Accomplishments
- App / Web / Social Media

**Chapter on Mission**

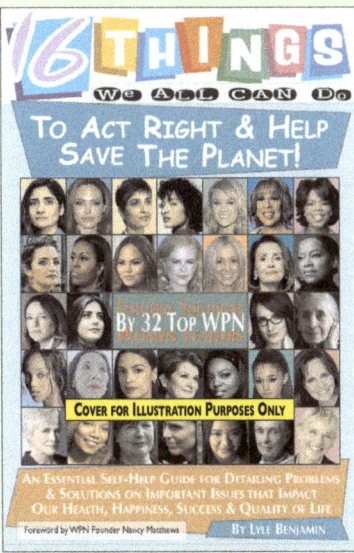

16 THINGS
We All Can Do
To Act Right & Help Save The Planet!
Featured Stories By 32 Top WPN Women Leaders
Cover For Illustration Purposes Only
An Essential Self-Help Guide for Detailing Problems & Solutions on Important Issues that Impact Our Health, Happiness, Success & Quality of Life.
Foreword by WPN Founder Nancy Matthews
By Lyle Benjamin

**~20,000**
Book Distribution

**1,000's** Attend Free
8-12 Week "One Planet One People" Book-Based Workshops

**Increased:**
| | |
|---|---|
| > Branding | > Publicity |
| > Marketing | > Philanthropy |
| > Media | > Revenue |

"What you're doing is great. I'm glad you're taking on this project. We definitely need it. We've become so, let's just call, divided in our country and when we are just talking being human beings, about solving problems we all share, it doesn't matter what side of the political spectrum you're on."
— **Jack Canfield**, Best-Selling Author of "Chicken Soup for the Soul" and "The Success Principles"

Planned Acts of Kindness • PlannedActs.Org
Lyle Benjamin, Founder • 212.213.0257

## Fund-Raising • Publicity • Engagement • Recruitment

# SIREM

## Social Institutional Reform & Equality Month

# SIREM

**FULL 31-DAY VIDEO, DISCUSSION & ACTION FORUMS AVAILABLE THRU PAK APP**

SIREM WORKS TO PROVIDE SCALABLE SOLUTIONS TO SOCIAL & ECONOMIC QUALITY OF LIFE ISSUES BASED ON THE **ONE PLANET ONE PEOPLE** PRINCIPLES OF CIVILITY, SOCIAL RESPONSIBILITY VOLUNTEERISM & GLOBAL CITIZENSHIP

WE INVITE YOU TO GET INVOLVED.

HELP US MAKE THE SOLUTIONS HAPPEN.

SIREM IS ALSO AVAILABLE AS A FULLY CUSTOMIZABLE PROGRAM FOR USE IN: SCHOOLS
• FAITH BASED & NPOS
• GOVERNMENTS
• BUSINESSES

**"TO MAKE THE CHANGE WE DESPERATELY NEED IN THE WORLD WE NEED ORDINARY PEOPLE DOING EXTRAORDINARY THINGS"**
**— LYLE BENJAMIN, FOUNDER PAK/IPOP**

| | | | |
|---|---|---|---|
| ☐ ONE PLANET ONE PEOPLE COURSE #1: CIVILITY **DAY 4** | ☐ INSTITUTIONAL REFORMS: FAITH-BASED ORGANIZATIONS **DAY 6** | ☐ RACE EQUALITY PANEL DISCUSSION. *PEACE COORDINATORS **DAY 7** | ☐ MONEY MATTERS MASTERY: FINANCIAL LITERACY & PLANNING **DAY 8** |
| ☐ ONE PLANET ONE PEOPLE COURSE #2: SOCIAL RESPONSIBILITY **DAY 11** | ☐ INSTITUTIONAL REFORMS: EDUCATION & PRACTICE **DAY 13** | ☐ WORKER & WEALTH EQUALITY PANEL DISCUSSION **DAY 14** | ☐ CAREER TRACK MANAGEMENT 8-FOUNDATION SKILLS **DAY 15** |
| ☐ ONE PLANET ONE PEOPLE COURSE #3: VOLUNTEERISM **DAY 18** | ☐ INSTITUTIONAL REFORMS: NON-PROFITS & NON-GOV'T ORGS **DAY 20** | ☐ HEALTH & WELLNESS EQUALITY PANEL DISCUSSIONS **DAY 21** | ☐ INTERNSHIP & MENTORSHIP CAREER TRAINING **DAY 22** |
| ☐ ONE PLANET ONE PEOPLE COURSE #4: GLOBAL CITIZENSHIP **DAY 25** | ☐ INSTITUTIONAL REFORMS: GLOBAL GOVERNMENTS **DAY 27** | ☐ RACIAL, RELIGIOUS GENDER EQUALITY PANEL DISCUSSIONS **DAY 28** | ☐ GLOBAL SOCIAL RESPONSIBILITY CAREER OPPORTUNITIES **DAY 29** |

# CALLING ALL SPEAKERS & ACTIVISTS!

**What's Your Cause?**
**Your Mission?**
**Your Passion?**

*Team up with*
*Planned Acts of Kindness*
*& One Planet One People*
*Programs & Initiatives*

# BE THE HERO & BE FEATURED IN BOOK, APP & EVENTS!

## SIREM
### Social Institutional Reform & Equality Month

## SIREM
## SPEAKS!
*People Providing Solutions*

# DAILY TALKS ON GLOBAL QUALITY OF LIFE ISSUES & SOLUTIONS

# CREATING LEGACIES FOR LOST LOVED ONES
## MEMORIAL BOOKS CAN BE BRANDED FOR ORGANIZATIONS AS GIVE-AWAYS

**ASK HOW PAK BOOKS CAN BE BRANDED TO EXCEED CSR OBJECTIVES AS WELL AS FUND-RAISING GOALS**

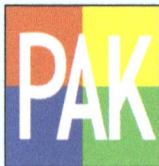

**PAK**

# HELP HEAL COVID-19 FAMILIES

COVID-19 has negatively impacted nearly everyone on this planet, none more so than the families that have lost loved ones. *Planned Acts of Kindness'* goal is to bring some degree of lasting peace to these families by giving them a *free Legacy Lifelines Memorial Book* to help keep the joy & the happiness of their loved one alive for generations to come.

# LEGACY LIFELINES
# Memorial

*Keeping the Joy & Happiness Alive for You,
Your Family & Generations to Come*

Dedicated to the lives lost from COVID-19

## By Lyle Benjamin
*Founder of Non-Profit Planned Acts of Kindness*

## A Special Message from Jack Canfield
*Best-Selling Author of Chicken Soup for the Soul*

**Mission:**
Help get books into the lives of individuals and families that lost loved ones due to C-19

**Take Action:**
Promote on Social Media to your connections and through others

Engage your schools, faith-based, non-profit orgs, businesses and governments to do book drives on a local, national & global level

Contact celebrities, influencers, athletes, teams, and leaders around the world and ask them to help spread the word

Donate a Legacy Memorial book to an individual or family that lost a loved one due to C-19

Help us locate and engage Sponsors, Partners, Donors both small, medium and large

Help bring Health, Happiness & Wellness into more people's lives through Project KOPE

80

# SECTION VIII: CAUSES & CAMPAIGNS

> "PASSION IS ENERGY. FEEL THE POWER THAT COMES FROM FOCUSING ON WHAT EXCITES YOU."
> — OPRAH WINFREY

# ONE TABLE ONE WORLD

## BRINGING PEOPLE TOGETHER THROUGH PLANNED ACTS OF FOOD

# WE LIVE IN GLORIOUS ISOLATION
## FAR REMOVED FROM THE INTIMATE FLAVORS of WORLD

# BUT SOME of THE BEST TIMES in OUR LIVES
## ARE THE ONES WE SPEND AROUND THE TABLE WITH FAMILY & FRIENDS

## GUESS WHO'S COMING TO DINNER?

*Cooking With Ria Trinidad*

# GET READY TO ROCK YOUR TASTE BUDS SILLY
## AS YOU BRING TO THE TABLE CUISINES, FAMILY & FRIENDS FROM AROUND THE WORLD

CELEBRITY CHEF PRESENTS

NEW MENU EVERY WEEK

5-7 DAYS LATER YOU COOK

SHARE 1POP COMMUNITY

## 6 CONTINENTS • 200+ COUNTRIES • THAT'S A WHOLE LOTTA JOY • PLANNEDACTS.ORG

AFRICA

ASIA

OCEANIA

EUROPE

N.AMERICA

S. AMERICA

# THE S.A.W. CHALLENGE
## CONNECTING PEOPLE WITH SMILES (CPS)

HELP LAUNCH THE MOST IMPORTANT REVOLUTION THE WORLD HAS EVER EXPERIENCED & IT ALL STARTS WITH YOU & A SMILE!

## "VENI, VIDI, CONNEXUM"
### I CAME ~ I S.A.W. ~ I CONNECTED

THAT'S ALL YOU HAVE TO DO:

### S.A.W. ~ SMILE & WAVE

SHARE YOUR SUCCESS STORIES
DO THE S.A.W. CHAIN CHALLENGE!

LIFE IS NOT ALWAYS EASY. WE ALL GET CAUGHT UP IN OUR DAY TO DAY & WE DON'T ALWAYS TAKE THE TIME TO BE GOOD TO OURSELVES OR KIND TO OTHERS

## WOULDN'T YOUR DAY BE A BIT NICER IF YOU GIVE & RECEIVE A FEW EXTRA SMILES & WAVES ALONG THE WAY?

IMAGINE ... STUDENTS AROUND THE WORLD STARTING & ENDING EACH CLASS
IMAGINE ... FAITH-BASED ORGS STARTING & ENDING CONGREGATIONS
IMAGINE ... COMPANIES STARTING & ENDING REMOTE & IN-PERSON MEETINGS
IMAGINE ... GOVERNMENT AGENCIES DOING THE SAME
IMAGINE ... SPORTING EVENTS WHERE THE ENTIRE STADIUM S.A.W.
IMAGINE ... KIDS, TEENS, ADULTS GREETING/LEAVING OTHERS WITH RESPECT, KINDNESS, GRATITUDE

## CHALLENGE YOUR GROUP • TAKE & POST PICTURES • ASK GROUP TO MAKE CHAINS ISSUE CHALLENGES • HOW MANY PEOPLE/COUNTRIES CAN YOU ENGAGE EVERY 30 DAYS?

IMAGINE ... IT STARTS WITH YOU & A RIPPLE. RIPPLES BECOME WAVES. WAVES BECOME TSUNAMIS OF CHANGE
IMAGINE ... IF WE ACT LIKE WE ARE ONE PLANET ONE PEOPLE? IT WILL BE A WONDERFUL WORLD (83)

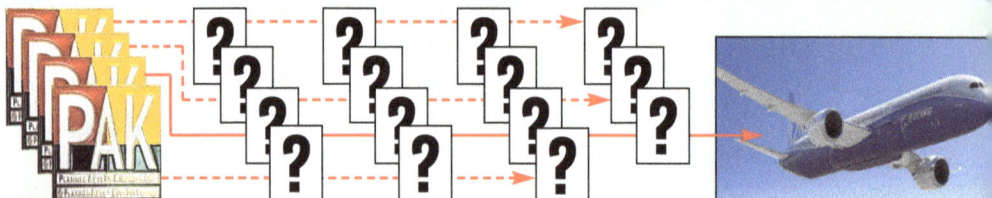

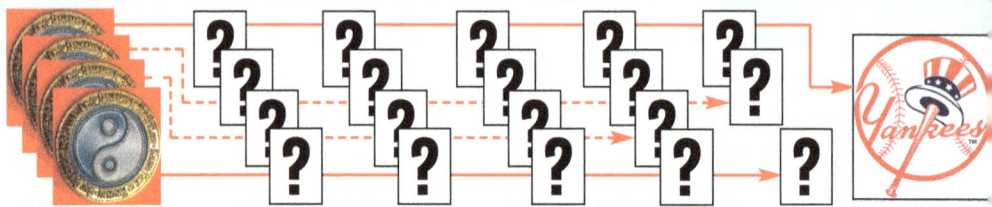

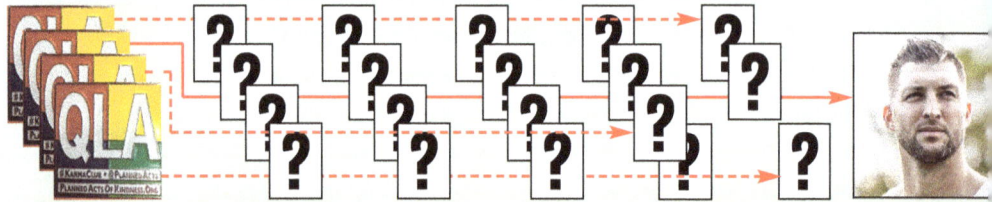

# TO SOLVE THE PROBLEMS OF THE WORLD WE MUST COME TOGETHER AS ONE PLANET ONE PEOPLE

**PAK**

## PLANNED ACTS OF KINDNESS INVITES YOU TO JOIN WITH PEOPLE ALL OVER THE WORLD IN TAKING

# THE GREAT PIZZA PEACE PLAN CHALLENGE

**Get The PAK App & Eat Pizza!**

JOIN MONTHLY GOLBAL PIZZA PARTIES!!

**Make Your Kindness Civility Pledge Video**

SHARE PAK/IPOP STORIES IN COMMUNITY

**Add Video Pledge To World Map & Challenge Others!**

COLLABORATE WITH NEW FRIENDS • BE THE HERO

**Peace Challenge:** "I hereby make a PAK to treat others with respect & kindness and to go through life from this day forward acting towards others as I would wish to be treated myself." *This is (name) from (city/country) for* PlannedActs.Org & One Planet One People

**2022-25 GOALS** | **200+ COUNTRIES** | **100'S OF MILLIONS ENGAGED**

**THE GREAT PIZZA**

**PEACE PLAN CHALLENGE**

*Prizes! • Global Pizza Peace Parties • Rewards!*

"I think we're going to need to order more pizza!"

"No problem. Magic delivers!"

# STEP UP, BE THE HERO!
**PROGRAMS FOR FAMILIES • FRIENDS • GROUPS • CLUBS TEAMS • SCHOOLS • ORGS • BUSINESSES • GOVERNMENTS** 85

WE MUST CREATE A WORLD WHERE WE ARE IN SYNC WITH THE PLANET. HUMANS ARE NOW THE PLANET'S EQUIVALENT OF COVID-19. CLIMATE CHANGE IS THE PLANET'S IMMUNE SYSTEM RAMPING UP TO WIPE OUT THE VIRUS: US.

FIND OUT HOW YOU CAN HELP!

GET PAK APP

## THE PEOPLE THAT BENEFIT THE MOST FROM THESE TURBULENT TIMES ARE THE WORLD'S BILLIONAIRES

### Worker Earnings vs. Billionaire Wealth

$4 T
$3 T
$2 T
$1 T
$0 T
$-1 T
$-2 T
$-3 T
$-4 T

BILLIONAIRE WEALTH GAINED +3.9 TRILLION

GLOBAL WORKER EARNINGS LOST -3.7 TRILLION

March 18 - Dec. 31, 2020

Source: Oxfam and the International Labour Organization

### 2021 WORLD'S BILLIONAIRES (FORBES)

| | |
|---|---|
| 2,755 | BILLIONAIRES |
| 660 | INCREASE OVER 2020 |
| 1 | NEW BILLIONAIRE EVERY 17 HOURS |
| 13.1 | TRILLION IN WORTH |
| 8 | TRILLION GAIN OVER 2020 |
| 86% | GAINED WEALTH DURING PANDEMIC |

INCOME INEQUALITY GROWTH (1% VS 90%) FROM 1975 TO 2020 COST AMERICAN WORKERS $50 TRILLION IN INCOME

THE DIFFERENCE: IF EARNING $35,000 TODAY YOU'D ADD $26,000 TO YOUR INCOME. EARN $72,000? YOU WOULD HAVE BEEN EARNING $48,000-$63,000 MORE. Source: Rand Corporation

THE WINDOW OF OPPORTUNITY TO STOP THE TIPPING POINTS & INEQUALITIES IS CLOSING. WE MUST STOP THE FRACTIONAL APPROACH TO SOLVING GLOBAL PROBLEMS & COLLABORATE ON AN INSTITUTIONAL BASIS ACROSS DISCIPLINES & COUNTRY BOUNDARIES

# LET'S ASK THE ONE PERCENTERS TO HELP ENSURE QUALITY OF LIFE FOR ONE PLANET ONE PEOPLE

## TEN RICHEST BILLIONAIRES: 2020: $686 BILLION 2021: $1.5 TRILLION

TRACK HOW BILLIONAIRES CARE ON THE PAK APP

| | | |
|---|---|---|
| 1. JEFF BEZOS $64 TO $177B | 2. ELON MUSK $24.6 TO $151B | 3. BERNARD ARNAULT $76 TO $150B | 4. BILL GATES $98 TO $124B |
| 5. MARK ZUCKERBERG $97B | 6. WARREN BUFFET $96B | 7. LARRY ELLISON $93B / 8. LARRY PAGE $91.5B | 9. SERGEY BRIN $89B / 10. MUKESH AMBANI $84B |

## 2022-24 GOALS   200+ COUNTRIES   100'S OF MILLIONS ENGAGED

- 20,000+ COLLABORATION PARTNERS
- 200 GOVT COLLABORATIONS
- 350 SDG INDUSTRY PARTNERS
- BOOKS, COURSES, WORKSHOPS
- SCALABLE ACTION PLANS SOCIAL, ECONOMIC, ENVIRON. ISSUES
- E-QL EDU FOR QUALITY OF LIFE
- ONE PLANET ONE PEOPLE CLUBS
- EDU & CAREER TRAINING PROGRAMS

# THE ULTIMATE VOLUNTEERING CHALLENGE:
# JOIN CAAP: CRAZY AMBITIOUS ACTIVITIES PROGRAM

**Crazy Ambitious Activities Program**

"To Make The Change We Desperately Need In The World We Need Ordinary People Doing Extraordinary Things."
— Lyle Benjamin, Founder PAK/1POP

This is **Volunteering at the Next Level** for people that want their actions to really make a difference on a major scale ...serving soup, cleaning parks, going on walks just don't cut it for this group. We have much **bigger Quality of Life** goals because we are capable of much, much more. We understand the clock is running and we have a limited window of opportunity to push back on the global issues that threaten the health and well-being of people all over the world. We are bringing action programs into our schools, faith-based orgs, non-profits, governments and our places of work so we can join together as **One Planet One People.**

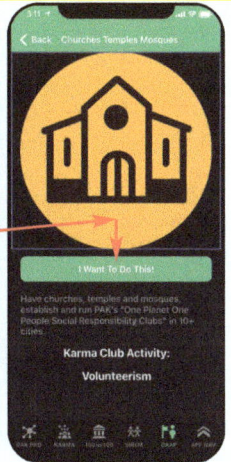

Have churches, temples and mosques establish and run PAK's "One Planet One People Social Responsibility Clubs" in 10+ cities.

**Karma Club Activity:**
Volunteerism

---

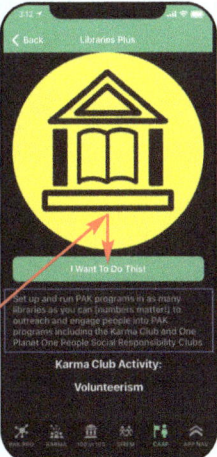

Set up and run PAK programs in as many libraries as you can [numbers matter!], to outreach and engage people into PAK programs including the Karma Club and One Planet One People Social Responsibility Clubs

**Karma Club Activity:**
Volunteerism

**STEP 1** — GET PAK APP

**STEP 2** — VISIT CAAP

**STEP 3** — READ, LOVE & CHOOSE!

**STEP 4** — DO ALONE OR WITH TEAM!

**STEP 5** — WE HELP MAKE IT HAPPEN

**STEP 6** — WE INTERVIEW YOU AS THE HERO TO INSPIRE OTHERS

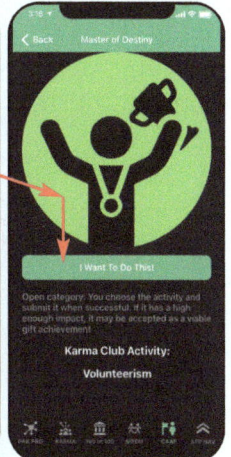

Open category: You choose the activity and submit it when successful. If it has a high enough impact, it may be accepted as a viable gift achievement

**Karma Club Activity:**
Volunteerism

---

Get a major sports league (NFL, MLB, MBA, NHL, MLS) to Sponsor PAK through team outreach, engagement events and promotions of stadiums, parks and website

**Karma Club Activity:**
Volunteerism

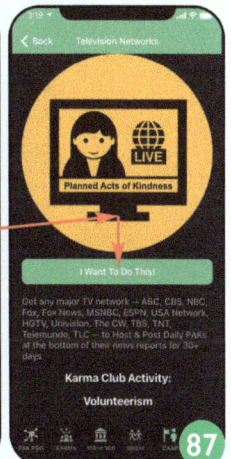

Get any major TV network – ABC, CBS, NBC, Fox, Fox News, MSNBC, ESPN, USA Network, HGTV, Univision, The CW, TBS, TNT, Telemundo, TLC – to Host & Post Daily PAKs at the bottom of their news reports for 30+ days

**Karma Club Activity:**
Volunteerism

# THE GLOBAL CAMPAIGN FOR KINDNESS

URGENT GLOBAL ALERT POSTED!

## INVOLVE YOUR SCHOOL, NON-PROFIT, COMPANY, TEAM, FAMILY, FRIENDS. STEP UP. BE THE HERO.

## CREATE PSA (PUBLIC SERVICE ANNOUNCEMENT) VIDEOS

### CAMPAIGN FOR KINDNESS!

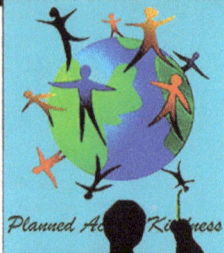

USE YOUR TALENT!

BE THE HERO!

SHARE A STORY!

TAKE THE PLEDGE!

PROMOTE PEACE!

CREATE A PSA!

EARN PRIZES!

FOR MORE INFORMATION VISIT OUR WEBSITE!

PAK "100 PSAs IN 100 DAYS"
PLANNEDACTSOFKINDNESS.ORG

### BE THE HERO!

SHOW THE WORLD WHAT YOU'VE GOT!

ALL AGES
ALL COUNTRIES
ALL LANGUAGES!

PLAY AN INSTRUMENT? SPORT? DANCE? SING? ACT? MAKE ART? FILMS?

VISIT OUR WEBSITE FOR MORE INFORMATION

SHOWCASE YOUR TALENTS & SEND US A VIDEO TO MAKE THE WORLD A BETTER PLACE!

EARN PRIZES!

PAK "100 PSAs IN 100 DAYS"
PLANNEDACTSOFKINDNESS.ORG

Checkout "100 PSAs" on PAK App

Make Your Kindness Video(s)!

Add To App, Share & Challenge Others!

### BE THE HERO!

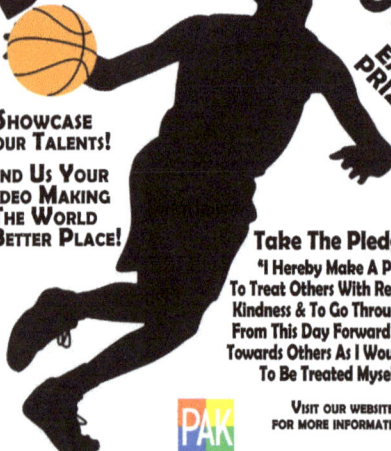

SHOWCASE YOUR TALENTS!

SEND US YOUR VIDEO MAKING THE WORLD A BETTER PLACE!

EARN PRIZES!

Take The Pledge:
"I Hereby Make A PAK To Treat Others With Respect & Kindness & To Go Through Life From This Day Forward Acting Towards Others As I Would Wish To Be Treated Myself."

VISIT OUR WEBSITE FOR MORE INFORMATION!

PAK

"100 PSAs IN 100 DAYS"
PLANNEDACTSOFKINDNESS.ORG

88

### THE CAMPAIGN FOR KINDNESS

STARTS NOW!

BE THE HERO!

SHARE A STORY OF HOW A PLANNED ACT OF KINDNESS CHANGED YOUR LIFE!

CREATE A PSA! EARN PRIZES!

For more information visit our website!

USE YOUR TALENTS!

PAK "100 PSAs IN 100 DAYS"
PLANNEDACTSOFKINDNESS.ORG

# SECTION IX:
# EXCEEDING CORPORATE/ORGANIZATIONAL OBJECTIVES

> "WITHOUT RESTORING AN ETHOS OF SOCIAL RESPONSIBILITY, THERE CAN BE NO MEANINGFUL AND SUSTAINED ECONOMIC RECOVERY."
> — JEFFREY SACHS

# HAVE CORPORATE/ORG OBJECTIVES?
## FROM A-Z — WE'VE GOT YOUR SOLUTIONS

CORPORATE 401K, 403B, 457 SUPPLEMENTAL CUSTOM BENEFIT PLANS

CORPORATE ADVERTISING, ACHIEVEMENTS, ARCHITECTURE, APPS & ACTION

CORPORATE BRANDING (APPS, BOOKS, CAMPAIGNS, COURSES, EVENTS, GAMES, PROGRAMS, WEB SITES, WORKSHOPS)

CORPORATE CULTURE, CHARITY, CONNECTIONS, COLLABORATIONS, CSR & CEOS

CORPORATE DEVELOPMENT & DESIGN

CORPORATE ENGAGEMENT, EVENTS, EDUCATION, ENTREPRENEURSHIP & EMPLOYEE BENEFITS

CORPORATE FINANCES & FUNDING

CORPORATE GLOBAL CITIZENSHIP, GREEN, GIFTS & GIVING

CORPORATE HIRING, HUMAN RESOURCES & HEALTHCARE

CORPORATE IDENTITY, INTEGRITY, INNOVATION, INCENTIVES, INSURANCE & INCOME

CORPORATE JOINT VENTURES & JOB SATISFACTION

CORPORATE KNOWLEDGE, KNOWHOW & KEYNOTE SPEAKER

CORPORATE LEADERSHIP & LEGACY

CORPORATE MISSION, MARKETING, MASTERMIND, MERCHANDIZING & MANAGEMENT TRAINING

CORPORATE NUMBERS, NEWSLETTER & NETWORKING

CORPORATE OUTREACH, OFFICES, ONBOARDING & OBJECTIVES

CORPORATE PUBLIC RELATIONS, PROMOTIONS, PERKS, PSAS, PARTNERSHIPS, PROFITS & PHILANTHROPY

CORPORATE QUOTAS, QUARTERS & QUESTS

CORPORATE RESPONSIBILITY, REPUTATION, RECORDS, RECRUITING/RETAINMENT & REVENUE

CORPORATE SUSTAINABILITY, STRATEGY, SOCIAL RESPONSIBILITY, SDGS, SOCIAL MEDIA & SPONSORSHIP

CORPORATE TRAINING, TEAM BUILDING, TRADE SHOWS & THINK TANK

CORPORATE UNIFORMS & UNDERSTANDING

CORPORATE VENTURES, VISION, VIDEOS & VOLUNTEERING

CORPORATE WELLNESS, WORKSHOPS, WEBSITES & WEALTH

CORPORATE XEROXING & XMAS

CORPORATE YOUTUBE, YOUTH PROGRAMS & FUNDING

CORPORATE ZEST!

ONE PLANET ONE PEOPLE · GLOBAL ACTION PROGRAMS · PLANIDEACTS.ORG

## ONE PLANET ONE PEOPLE
### MAKING THE WORLD A BETTER PLACE, ONE PAK AT A TIME

# SPONSORSHIPS · PARTNERSHIPS
## OUTREACH • SOCIAL RESPONSIBILITY ENGAGEMENT • REVENUE

## HOW TO STAND OUT FROM THE CROWD IS HARDER THAN EVER BEFORE

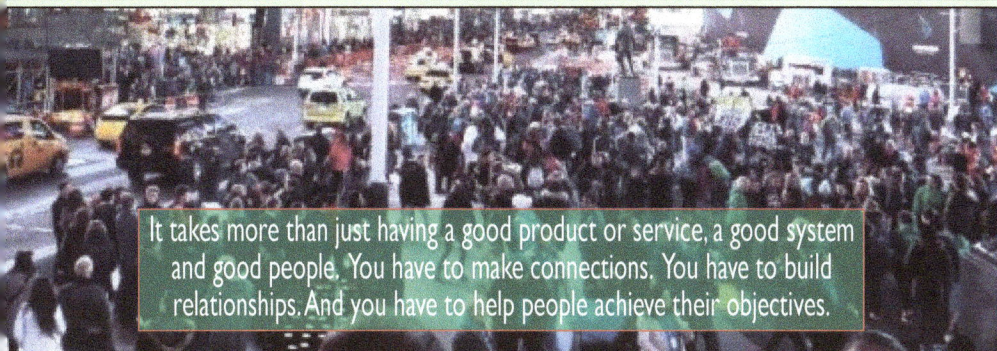

It takes more than just having a good product or service, a good system and good people. You have to make connections. You have to build relationships. And you have to help people achieve their objectives.

## OUR PROGRAMS HELP YOU (1) MAKE CONNECTIONS; (2) BUILD RELATIONSHIPS; (3) ACHIEVE OBJECTIVES, SO YOU CAN STAND OUT FROM THE CROWD & DO WHAT YOU DO BEST

### 1. MAKING CONNECTIONS
USE OUR SOCIAL RESPONSIBILITY PROGRAMS TO MAKE CONNECTIONS WITH YOUR TARGET AUDIENCES

When your prospects, clients, customers and staff learn about the work that we do: Our books, workshops, programs and activities to help achieve better "Quality of Life" for People and the Planet … it resonates. It connects. And the company or organization that helps make the connection by supporting our programs, gains the goodwill of the people who see the connection as well as those on the receiving end.

### 2. BUILDING RELATIONSHIPS
WE SHOW YOUR CONNECTIONS HOW WE CAN HELP THEM ACHIEVE THEIR OBJECTIVES & IT BENEFITS YOU

You are the referral that makes the introduction. Our Social Responsibility books, workshops, programs, activities and initiatives help build the relationship. Your association with us and referral reinforces the impression that your company cares enough to share and support something of value to them that doesn't directly tie into your bottom line. Positive association and goodwill are very powerful drivers in a crowded market.

### 3. Achieving Objectives
USING OUR SOCIAL RESPONSIBILITY PROGRAMS TO ACHIEVE YOUR, THEIR & OUR SHARE/STAKEHOLDER GOALS

Our Mission is to help people lead "Happier, Healthier & More Successful Lives." We do this by collaborating with schools, orgs, govt and companies, helping them achieve their objectives in conjunction with our programs — that's why we have six different delivery systems with dozens of initiatives all geared to accomplish one thing: Quality of Life for All. Our relationship building system creates Win-Win-Win outcomes where everyone involved benefits.

## CO-BRANDING, ADVERTISING, MARKETING, PUBLIC RELATIONS & CSR IN BOOKS, COURSES, SUMMITS, WORKSHOPS, GAMES, PRODUCTS & INITIATIVES FOR ENHANCED OUTREACH, ENGAGEMENT, INSPIRATION & ACTION

## NOT A BAD POSITION TO BE IN WHEN YOU WANT TO STAND OUT IN A CROWD.

### CUSTOM PACKAGES TAILORED TO MEET YOUR OBJECTIVES
• BOOKS, COURSES, PROGRAMS, EVENTS, INITIATIVES: CLIENTS, PROSPECTS, EMPLOYEES
• LONG-LASTING BOOK BRANDING WITH ENGAGING MULTI-WEEK WORKSHOPS
• CSR TO IMPACT SHAREHOLDERS/STAKEHOLDERS & RECRUIT/RETAIN EMPLOYEES
• BRANDED SOCIAL & INSTITUTIONAL PROGRAMS WITH APP & EVENT TIE-INS
• FOUNDER LEVEL ACCESS, MASTERMIND SESSIONS, SPEAKING ENGAGEMENTS

### THE NEXT STEP:
### SHARE WITH US
### YOUR CSR OBJECTIVES

# HOW KINDNESS & CIVILITY CAN TURN BACK THE TIPPING POINTS & SAVE THE HUMAN RACE FROM SELF-DESTRUCTION

**LYLE BENJAMIN**
Activist, Entrepreneur, Speaker

Lyle Benjamin has been on a journey to repay others for the kindness he received while working in New York City at the age of 11. Ten years later he was in law school interning with the New York State Attorney General's Office in the Litigation Bureau writing Memorandums of Law on Public Health and other issues. But Benjamin concluded that the profession would force him to act like a hired gun, so he decided to help others by going in a different direction.

Following his undergraduate interests in writing, Benjamin went into the marketing, design and printing field. Shortly thereafter, he became the only person ever to have published a national newsstand magazine and a best-selling board game at the same time. Both the magazine and the game dealt with helping improve people's quality of life by improving their relationships.

In 2019, Benjamin created the 501(c)3 educational not-for-profit **Planned Acts of Kindness** with the objective of providing Quality of Life for everyone by developing a more unified world by gamifying Karma and instilling a greater sense of civility, social responsibility, volunteerism and global citizenship in people.

In 2021, Benjamin launched **One Planet One People** first as an environment platform, and then as an umbrella movement fully aligned with all 17 Sustainable Development Goals of the United Nations to unite people and institutions around the globe on tipping point and quality of life issues that require immediate global action.

Both organizations have earned the praises of schools, faith-based organizations, non-profits, government agencies and businesses including Google, the Peace Corps, Simon Property Group, and Jack Canfield, Best-Selling author of *Chicken Soup for the Soul* and *The Success Principles*.

Benjamin is the author of several non-fiction personal development books including *ONE: The Fight For Survival Of The Human Race; 16 Things We All Can Do To Act Right & Help Save The Planet!; The Working Dead: The Essential Survival Guide on How to Protect, Save & Invest for yourself, Your Family & Your Future;* and *Legacy Lifelines: Memorial Edition: Creating Legacies for Lost Loved Ones.* Benjamin's goal is to collaborate with organizations and governments around the world to give a free memorial book to every family that lost a loved one due to COVID-19 to help with them with the healing process.

## SPEAKER, STORY & WORKSHOP IDEAS

✓ **How To Prevent The Fractional Approach Companies & Governments Use To Solve Global Issues From Ending Human Life**

✓ **How Companies Can Use Corporate Social Responsibility (CSR) To Create Work/Life Balance For Employees** To Keep Them From Walking Off The Job

✓ **Learn The 6 Tipping Points That Can End Us & The One Thing We Have To Do To Save Us**

✓ **Want to Live a Longer Life? Hint: It Has Nothing To Do With Medicine or Exercise**

✓ **How Doing a Daily Planned Act of Kindness Can Make Can Make You The Hero That Saves The Planet**

✓ **How To Convince Your Boss That Paying You To Volunteer Is Really Smart Business**

Your Guide to the Collaborative Programs & Initiatives Needed to Help Solve Social, Environmental & Economic Issues on a Local to Global Scale at your Company, Farm-Based or Non-Profit Organization, Gov't Agency, School, Network or Home

# ONE
## The Fight for Survival of the Human Race

By Lyle Benjamin with Alice Mok

Founder of One Planet One People, Planned Acts of Kindness & the Collaboration Think Tank Network

**BY LYLE BENJAMIN**
Author, Educator, Financial Advisor

✓ **3 Things We Can Do Today To Help Heal The Rift Between People & Police**

✓ **Your Voice Matters, But Actions Speak Louder:** How Doing Daily Planned Acts of Kindness Can Change the World

✓ **Want To Save The Planet? Do These 3 Things Starting Today**

## YOUR GUIDE TO THE COLLABORATIVE INITIATIVES NEEDED TO HELP SOLVE SOCIAL, ENVIRONMENTAL & ECONOMIC ISSUES

UNITED NATIONS · COLUMBIA UNIVERSITY · PEACE CORPS · POLICE PAL · MIT · WESLEYAN COLLEGE · LIBERTY TAX SERVICE · THE NEW YORK STATE SENATE

NATIONAL & INTERNATIONAL • SHORT NOTICE • NYC BASED • 917 683-2625 • LyleBenjamin@PlannedActs.Org
PlannedActs.Org • OnePlanet-OnePeople.Com • LegacyLineClubs.Com • TheWorkingDead.Us

# HR to CSR: Talks, Workshops, Events
## How to "Act & Grow Rich" with Money Matters Mastery
### From Game Changing Financial Concepts to Custom Benefits

## The Measure Of A Person's Wealth Is Not How Much You Make, It's How Much You Get To Keep

Lyle Benjamin has been an entrepreneur since his college days. He owns the distinction of being the only person ever to have been the publisher of a national newsstand magazine and a best-selling board game at the same time.

In 2019, Benjamin created the 501(c)3 educational not-for-profit **Planned Acts of Kindness** with the objective of providing Quality of Life for everyone by developing a more unified world by gamifying Karma and instilling a greater sense of civility, social responsibility, volunteerism and global citizenship in people.

### LYLE BENJAMIN
Activist, Entrepreneur, Speaker

In 2021, Benjamin launched **One Planet One People** first as an environment platform, and then as an umbrella movement fully aligned with all 17 Sustainable Development Goals of the United Nations to unite people and institutions around the globe on tipping point and quality of life issues that require immediate global action.

Both organizations have earned the praises of schools, faith-based organizations, non-profits, government agencies and businesses including Google, the Peace Corps, Simon Property Group, and Jack Canfield, Best-Selling author of *Chicken Soup for the Soul* and *The Success Principles*.

In keeping with his mission of helping people, Benjamin created the educational program *Money Matters Mastery* to educate people on financial literacy and planning, so they can better provide for themselves, their families and their futures.

Benjamin is the author of several non-fiction personal development books including *The Working Dead: The Essential Survival Guide on How to Protect, Save & Invest for yourself, Your Family & Your Future; ONE: The Fight For Survival Of The Human Race; 16 Things We All Can Do To Act Right & Help Save The Planet!* and *Legacy Lifelines: Memorial Edition: Creating Legacies for Lost Loved Ones.* Benjamin's goal is to collaborate with organizations and governments around the world to give a free memorial book to every family that lost a loved one due to COVID-19 to help with them with the healing process.

## SPEAKER, STORY & WORKSHOP IDEAS

✓ **How Companies Can Use Corporate Social Responsibility (CSR) To Create Work/Life Balance For Employees** To Keep Them From Walking Off The Job

✓ **Four Things Every Employee Should Ask Their Company To Do Right Away,** That Can Increase Profitability, Lower Expenses & Keep Employees Happy

✓ **4 Keys To Help Employees Get Greater Financial Benefits** & Become More Productive & Loyal To Your Company

✓ **The 4 Ways Your 401K Fails You** & The One Thing That The Rich Do That Can Save You

✓ **How Health Care Costs Can Bankrupt You** & What You Need To Do Now To Protect Yourself & Your Family Before It's Too Late

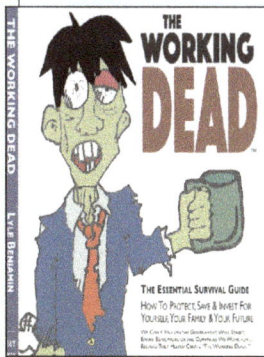

✓ **4 Mistakes Families Make In Building For Their Future** & The 4 Things They Have To Start Doing Right Away

✓ **Why Our Institutions Are Designed To Fail Us** & The 4 Things Everyone Must Do To Live Happier, Healthier & More Successful Lives

✓ **Why Your College Degree Deserves A "D"** & What You Need To Do To Raise Your Grade

### THE WORKING DEAD
THE WORKING DEAD
LYLE BENJAMIN

How To Protect, Save & Invest For Yourself, Your Family & Your Future

### BY LYLE BENJAMIN
Author, Educator, Financial Advisor

**THE ESSENTIAL "MONEY BOOK" THAT EVERYONE NEEDS TO READ & ACT ON, REGARDLESS OF EDUCATION OR INCOME**

UNITED NATIONS · G · COLUMBIA UNIVERSITY · PEACE CORPS · POLICE ATHLETIC LEAGUE · MIT · THE WESLEYAN CHURCH · LIBERTY TAX SERVICE · THE NEW YORK STATE SENATE

# SUCCESS: INNOVATE OR DIE
**FIGURATIVELY... THEN LITERALLY**

## HOW PAK/IPOP FOUNDER, LYLE BENJAMIN, CAN TRANSFORM YOUR ORG

**WHETHER YOU HAVE A BUSINESS, SCHOOL, NPO, FAITH-BASED ORG OR GOVERNMENT AGENCY, YOU HAVE OBJECTIVES YOU WANT TO REACH**

 BUSINESS
 SCHOOL
 NPOs/NGOs
 FAITH-BASED
 GOVT/AGENCY

- **RESONATING MARKETING & PR CAMPAIGNS**
- **GAMIFICATION FOR BETTER ENGAGEMENT**
- **CORPORATE SOCIAL RESPONSIBILITY IMPACT**
- **INDEPENDENT REVIEW/ANALYSIS/INNOVATION**
- **MARKET EXPANSION**
- **NEW REVENUE STREAMS**
- **SDG INTEGRATION**
- **BETTER RECRUITMENT/RETAINMENT**

 SEE ONE BOOK PAGE 94 APP

**HOW YOU ACHIEVE THESE OBJECTIVES CAN TAKE MANY PATHS –**

**MARKETING, ADVERTISING, BRANDING, PUBLIC RELATIONS. BOOKS, COURSES, WEB SITES, APPS, VIDEOS, GAMES, PRODUCTS. PROGRAMS, CAMPAIGNS, EVENTS, SYSTEMS, PARTNERSHIPS.**

**INVOLVE COUNTLESS PEOPLE, TAKE MONTHS TO DEVELOP, AND COST HUNDREDS OF THOUSANDS TO MILLIONS OF DOLLARS, JUST IN PLANNING ALONE**

MEET PAK FOUNDER LYLE BENJAMIN → RECEIVE, SHARE & APPROVE PROPOSAL → RECEIVE FULLY SCALEABLE DELIVERABLE

**WHAT IF YOU COULD STREAMLINE THE ENTIRE PROCESS AND SAVE TIME, RESOURCES & MONEY, WHILE ...**

- **EMBRACING INNOVATION**
- **INCREASING ENGAGEMENT**
- **EXCEEDING OBJECTIVES**
- **BOOSTING BOTTOM LINE**

**94 WOULD THAT BE WORTH AN HOUR OF YOUR TIME & FEW BUCKS?**

# SECTION X:
# COMING SOON WITH A LITTLE
# HELP FROM OUR FRIENDS

ONE PLANET ONE PEOPLE SUMMITS:
GALVANIZING THE COLLABORATION COMMUNITY FOR QUALITY OF LIFE FOR ALL
96

"NONE OF US, INCLUDING
ME, EVER DO GREAT THINGS.
BUT WE CAN ALL DO SMALL
THINGS, WITH GREAT LOVE,
AND TOGETHER WE CAN DO
SOMETHING WONDERFUL."
— MOTHER TERESA

ONE PLANET ONE PEOPLE: THE FIGHT FOR SURVIVAL OF THE HUMAN RACE.
THE SOCIAL RESPONSIBILITY GAME THAT SHOWS WHAT OUR FUTURE MAY BE LIKE
& HOW YOU CAN COLLABORATE TO ENSURE QUALITY OF LIFE FOR BILLIONS
97

ONE PLANET ONE PEOPLE PORTAL: CONNECTING PEOPLE
TO COLLABORATIVE QUALITY OF LIFE GLOBAL SYSTEMS
98

COMMUNITY PARTNERSHIP CENTERS:
STRENGTHENING COMMUNITIES BY TRANSFORMING LIVES
99

You Are
Invited to Attend
**PLANNED ACTS OF KINDNESS'**

# 2022-25
# ONE PLANET
# ONE PEOPLE
# SUMMITS

**STREAMING LIVE & RECORDED**
**DATES & LOCATIONS UPDATED ON PAK APP**

**TOPICS OF DISCUSSION:** COLLABORATION THINK TANK TEAMS; SIREM & SIREM SPEAKERS; THE 4 PILLARS OF ONE PLANET ONE PEOPLE: CIVILITY, ETHICS, SOCIAL RESPONSIBILITY, GLOBAL CITIZENSHIP; E-QL EDUCATION-QUALITY OF LIFE; 1POP CLUBS; 16 BOOKS; WORKSHOPS; PROJECT KOPE; CAAP & MUCH MORE!

## Program & Speakers via App

**TED Talkers, Authors, Educators, Celebs**
**Workshops • Books • Prizes • Media**

## Sponsors

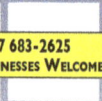

TO COLLABORATE CALL 917 683-2625
SCHOOLS • ORGS • GOV'T • BUSINESSES WELCOME

BRAHMA KUMARIS

PLANNED ACTS IS A 501(c)3 NON-PROFIT ORGANIZATION
SUPPORT@PLANNEDACTS.ORG • 212.213.0257

# PLANNEDACTSOFKINDNESS.ORG
Making the World a Better Place, One PAK at a Time

**ONE PLANET ONE PEOPLE EVENT SITES: SEE APP FOR MORE DETAILS & TO ADD YOUR CITY/TOWN**

**VOLUNTEERS, PARTNERS, SPONSORS WELCOME • RSVP VIA APP • LIVE STREAMED WORLDWIDE**

# SEE WHAT OUR FUTURE MAY BE LIKE & YOU MAY
## NOT LIKE WHAT YOU SEE. BUT YOU GOT WHAT IT TAKES TO CHANGE IT?

**IT'S MORE THAN A GAME WHEN BILLIONS OF LIVES ARE AT RISK**

# ONE PLANET-ONE PEOPLE
## THE FIGHT FOR SURVIVAL OF THE HUMAN RACE

**The World is in Crisis:** CLIMATE CHANGE, POLLUTION, PANDEMICS, TERRORISM & WAR
ARE YOU FRUSTRATED, SCARED, ANGRY at the direction our country — the planet — is headed?

In 10-20 Years the Tipping Points won't matter ... They will have already passed.
It's More Than A Game When Billions Of Lives Are At Risk!

BECOME A PART OF THE SOLUTION: JOIN THE KARMA REVOLUTION & HELP SAVE HUMANITY!
WHAT YOU DO TODAY MATTERS! The Time To Act Is Now!

**BE THE HERO & PARTNER WITH PEOPLE AROUND THE WORLD TO SAVE HUMANITY AS YOU BATTLE THE PLAGUES OF MANKIND**

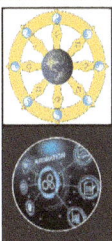

**OVERVIEW:**
Select your team from countries around the world and unite with other members of the Karma Club in the race to save humanity from extinction.

**BATTLE FACTIONS:**
It's the battle between the forces of Ethics, Social Responsibility and Global Citizenship Vs. Individual & Corporate Greed, Unbridled Tech and Governmental Power.

**REAL WORLD TIE-INs, PRIZES:**
What you do in the game doesn't just stay in the game — it has life-changing implications in your community and the world.

**An Education & Action Game for 2-8 Players, Ages 10-Adult. 75-120 minutes.**

**Game Play:** Join forces with other Karma Club Members around the world while battling other factions in order to save the Human Race from the Six Deadly Plagues. **To Win & Save The Human Race:** Position Karma Coalitions on all continents around the world before the 10-year Tipping Points window closes. (20 rounds)

**Components:**
- 12" x 12" Box
- 24" x 24" Board
- Rules
- 170 Country Coins
- 2 Dice
- On-Line Tie-Ins
- Free Offers
- Discount Offers
- Rewards & Prizes
- Program Guide

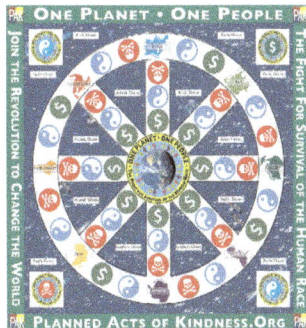

**AVAILABLE: DECEMBER 2022**

**Global Engagement:**
- Media Campaigns
- 2022: The Year of One Planet One People
- PAK/The Karma Club
- NPO/NGOs
- Schools/Universities
- Faith-Based Orgs
- Government Agencies
- Businesses
- Co-Branding
- Product Placement
- Sponsors/Fund-Raising

Proceeds help support the Missions of One Planet One People & Planned Acts of Kindness • PlannedActs.Org
Order On-Line • OnePlanet-OnePeople.Com • Sponsors Welcome • A New Game by Author, Educator: Lyle Benjamin

97

# COMMUNITY PARTNERSHIP CENTERS
## STRENGTHENING COMMUNITIES BY TRANSFORMING LIVES

**BE THE HERO IN YOUR COMMUNITY:**
FAMILIES • FRIENDS
PARTNERS

**OWN YOUR CTR**
FULL TRAINING
3 MONTHS

Individuals
Families
COMMUNITY PARTNERSHIP CENTERS
Businesses
Organizations

FULL NPO SUPPORT
GOVT REGULATED, LICENSED

HIGH REVENUE / INCOME
LOW STARTUP COSTS

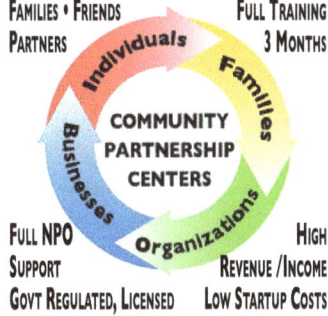

**PROVIDING A NETWORK OF ESSENTIAL SOCIAL RESPONSIBILITY PROGRAMS & SERVICES**

PAK

ONE PLANET ONE PEOPLE

**SERVING STUDENTS, EMPLOYEES, OWNERS, RETIREES & THE UNEMPLOYED**

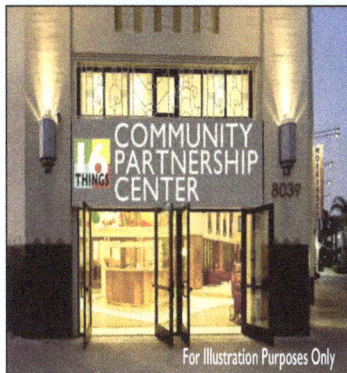

14 THINGS
COMMUNITY PARTNERSHIP CENTER
8039

For Illustration Purposes Only

**PARTNERING WITH LOCAL ORGANIZATIONS THAT GLADLY REFER PEOPLE**

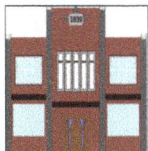

## HELPING PEOPLE OF ALL AGES CONNECT THE PIECES ... SO THEY CAN LEAD HAPPIER, HEALTHIER & MORE SUCCESSFUL LIVES

| EDUCATION | WORK | HEALTH | INCOME | PROTECTION | LEGAL | DEBT | SAVINGS | TAXES | RETIREMENT |

## HOW CAN WE HELP IMPROVE YOUR LIFE, OR THE LIFE OF SOMEONE YOU CARE ABOUT?

- ❏ After School / Weekend Club Programs
- ❏ Business Ownership Opportunities
- ❏ Business Services
- ❏ Career Track Services & Training
- ❏ Chronic & Long-Term Care Coverage
- ❏ Community Outreach Programs
- ❏ Computer Tech Services
- ❏ Custom Benefit Plans for Employers
- ❏ Debt Reduction & Management
- ❏ Educational Programs
- ❏ Employee Benefit Programs
- ❏ Entrepreneurial Programs
- ❏ Financial Consultation & Planning Services

- ❏ Fund-Raising Programs
- ❏ Health & Wellness Programs
- ❏ Health Coverage
- ❏ Insurance Needs
- ❏ Internship/Mentorship Programs
- ❏ Legal Advice & Protections
- ❏ Retirement Review & Planning
- ❏ Revenue Generation Programs
- ❏ Savings Programs
- ❏ Tax Reduction Programs
- ❏ Volunteer Programs
- ❏ Work & Career Programs
- ❏ Youth "Learn & Earn" Programs

PROGRAMS

ACTIVITIES

WORKSHOPS

CONSULTATION

**WANTED:**
- **PEOPLE WHO CARE**
- **EDUCATORS**
- **ACTIVISTS/LEADERS**
- **ENTREPRENEURS**

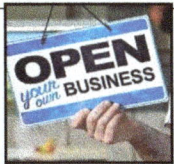

OPEN your own BUSINESS

**OWN YOUR CENTER. GO FROM EMPLOYEE TO OWNER IN 3 MONTHS**
COMMUNITY PARTNERSHIP CENTERS • NO EXP. REQUIRED
ALL TRAINING PROVIDED • LOW INVESTMENT & OVERHEAD
ASK ABOUT VETERAN, MINORITY & WOMEN PROGRAMS

VISIT OUR APP • SUPPORT@PLANNEDACTS.ORG • THEWORKINGDEAD.US • LYLE BENJAMIN, FOUNDER  99

# SECTION XI:
# SUPPORT & DONATIONS

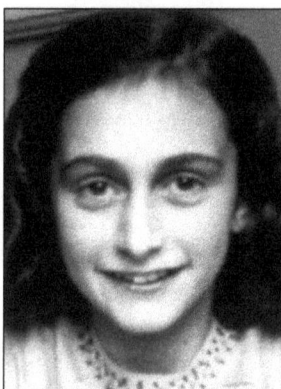

> "NO ONE HAS EVER
> BECOME POOR
> FROM GIVING."
> — ANNE FRANK

# IMAGE GALLERY
## A SAMPLING OF SUPPORT FOR PLANNED ACTS PROGRAMS

101

Google

SIMON PROPERTY GROUP

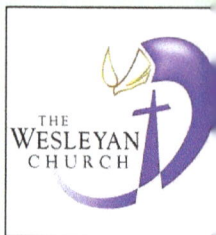

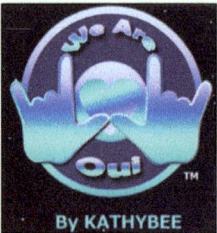

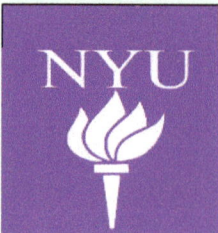

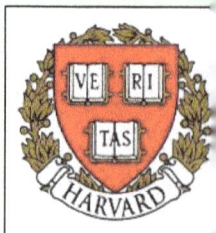

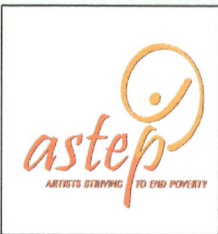

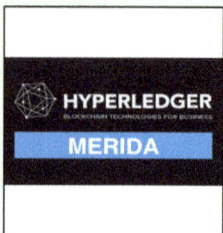

Peace Corps

UNITED NATIONS

HEARTS OF EMPOWERMENT

International Ahimsa Foundation

COLUMBIA UNIVERSITY

Teaching Children Serving Families

BRAHMA KUMARIS

POLICE ATHLETIC LEAGUE PAL NYC

MiT Massachusetts Institute of Technology

footsteps2brilliance — Big Brains for Little People

THE WESLEYAN CHURCH

We Are Oui By KATHYBEE

NYU

LISH HEALTH SERVICES

VERITAS HARVARD

BOSTON UNIVERSITY

astep — ARTISTS STRIVING TO END POVERTY

NYDJ FIT IS EVERYTHING

ALEX AND ANI — CHARITY BY DESIGN

WPN

IYP — INTERNATIONAL YOUTH PARLIAMENT

HYPERLEDGER — BLOCKCHAIN TECHNOLOGIES FOR BUSINESS — MERIDA

**TheStreet.**

**CISION**
PR Newswire

**euro news.**

**REAL SIMPLE**

**Daily Herald**
Big Picture . Local Focus

**finanzen.net**

**((·SiriusXM·))**

**abc NEWS**

**Life&Style** WEEKLY

**REDBOOK** .org.au

**GOOD MORNING AMERICA** abc

**Parents**

**Self**

**Kake News** abc

**Ladies' Home Journal**

**Entrepreneur MAGAZINE**

**Women'sHealth**

**e essence**

**Inc.**

**DAILY NEWS**
NYDAILYNEWS.COM

# "WE NEED YOUR HELP. BUT I PROMISED MY- SELF I WOULDN'T ASK

for contributions until I felt we had enough systems in place to really make a difference in the world. It took me over 11 years, but here we are. It hasn't been easy, along the way I made a lot of sacrifices, got divorced and battled long COVID.

Throughout the journey, I listened to the pulse of people and the planet, and added greater and greater depth and scope to our programs and initiatives. Now it's time to put the programs in place and start helping people on a massive scale, and I need your help to make it happen.

Can you spare an hour or so a week to share our programs? It's really kind of important and we make it really simple for you to do. There's absolutely no explaining, selling, persuading, crying or bullying involved. But there are rewards!"

Lyle Benjamin, Founder
Planned Acts of Kindness
One Planet One People

# DONATIONS & SUPPORT

### SUPPORT THE ONLY NPO ON THE PLANET WITH THE SCALEABLE SYSTEMS & COLLABORATIVE GLOBAL PROGRAMS THAT CAN HELP ACHIEVE THE 17 UN SDGS

*We could have taken the easy route and shown you pictures of disadvantaged children that need your support ... but when have we ever taken the easy way over the (albeit more wordy) better way?*

## WHY SUPPORT PAK & ONE PLANET ONE PEOPLE?

A Few Important Considerations:
1. You Get to Help Support Kids, People & the Planet in Times of Need
2. It Gives You a Stake in the Social Solutions to Our Problems
3. Provides People with the Strength to Do the Things They Can't Do Individually
4. Gives People Hope for a Brighter Future
5. Give People Purpose by Providing the Structure to Act on Social Issues
6. Affords People with a Safe Place to Strive for Social Good
7. Presents and Rewards Creativity in Working to Solve Issues
8. Successfully Allows for the Implementation of Innovation without Bowing to Profit

## YOUR DONATION REALLY MATTERS.

Every dollar you give helps us fund our collaborative education and action programs. Programs that work with five groups of people from the grassroots up and the five types of institutions from the top down to solve global issues that negatively affect Quality of Life for kids, people and the planet. And that means you, your family and your future generations yet to come ...

## YOUR DONATION. YOUR CHOICE. YOUR IMPACT.

Your donation isn't about us. It's about you and how you want to make an impact in the world. We're here to give you some options, and then of course, to make things happen on your behalf.

**PLEASE DONATE**
THRU THE PAK APP

| PLANNED ACTS OF KINDNESS | ONE PLANET ONE PEOPLE | 16 THINGS KIDS CAN DO |
|---|---|---|
| If kindness is your thing — this here's where it's at! | Global issues require scaleable/collaborative programs where all work as one. | No matter how old we are, what level of education or income, we can learn/do more. |
| • The Karma Club<br>• E-QL Kindness in Schools<br>• Project KOPE<br>• PAK in Prisons<br>• Funding Civility/Kindness Action Initiatives<br>• Crazy Ambitious Activities Programs (CAAP) | • One Planet One People Collaboration Campaign<br>• IPOP Clubs<br>• IPOP 4 Pillars Course<br>• SIREM & SIREM Speaks<br>• IPOP Global Portal<br>• IPOP Workshops | • 16 Things We All Can Do Education & Action Books<br>• Internships/Mentorships<br>• Career Training<br>• Money Matters Mastery<br>• Financial Literacy & Planning Programs |

## ADDITIONAL PROGRAMS & CAMPAIGNS

- 100 in 100 Days Collaboration Campaign
- The Great Pizza Peace Plan Challenge
- Project KOPE Health, Happiness & Wellness
- Global Peace Laureate Program
- IPOP Global Communication Portal
- Legacy Lifelines Memorial Book
  - PAK/IPOP Public Relations Campaign
  - NPR - National Public Radio Campaign

## TARGETED DONATIONS GO TOWARDS ACHIEVING GOALS

- Goal: 10,000 Institutions Worldwide 2025
- Goal: PAK Pledge & 8 Billion Planned Acts of Kindness by 2025
- Goal: Establish Programs in Schools, Faith-Based Orgs, Companies
- Goal: Establish 800 Youth/Adults 200 Countries/Promote Collaboration
- Goal: Connecting People to Collaborative Programs
- Goal: Give Book to Every Family Lost Loved One Due to COVID 19
- Goal: Hire PR Agency to Secure TV, Radio, Print Media Placement
- Goal: Engaging with Activist Audience to Expand Network

# DoNation "Hero" Packages

## How to Be a Nation of Doers: For Others, Your Country & the Planet

To Provide the Programs, Services & Initiatives We Do, It Requires Your Help. Simply Put, the More We Receive the More We're Able to Be of Service.

**Kinda Like Karma.**

Since We're All About the Positive Aspects of Karma ... When You Donate, What Goes Around Comes Around ... We Apply this to You Too!

**A** **Traditional Donation:** Go to our App, Enter the Amount You Wish to Donate & Select Monthly or Annually. Done. Well, Not Quite. Go Into Your Karma Club Account & Record Your Donation. Now You Just Earned Karma Credit, Too! In the U.S., Your Donation is Tax Deductible in Accordance with Your Taxes. Other Countries, Please Check Tax Code.

**B** **Donation Packages:** The Payment Process is the Same, But with Packages You Choose Your Rewards Right Away! Depending on Your Personal Situation, There Are Many Creative Ways You Can Use Packages to "Be The Hero" You're Receiving Goods in Exchange for Payment, So Only 50% of Your Payment May Be Considered as a Tax Donation.

### Significant Other Package

| Qty | Item | Price |
|---|---|---|
| 2 | ONE Books | $ 60.00 |
| 10 | IPOP Stickers | 5.00 |
| 4 | Wristbands | 14.00 |
| 4 | Karma Coins | 20.00 |
| 2 | PAK Pins | 20.00 |
| 2 | QLA Pins | 20.00 |
| 2 | WAM! Mugs | 50.00 |
|  | Subtotal | $ 189.00 |
|  | 10% Discount | 18.90 |
|  | Total Due | $ 170.10 |

### Special Occasion Package

| Qty | Item | Price |
|---|---|---|
| 4 | ONE Books | $ 120.00 |
| 50 | IPOP Stickers | 25.00 |
| 8 | Wristbands | 28.00 |
| 8 | Karma Coins | 40.00 |
| 4 | PAK Pins | 40.00 |
| 4 | QLA Pins | 40.00 |
| 4 | WAM! Mugs | 100.00 |
|  | Subtotal | $ 393.00 |
|  | 15% Discount | 58.95 |
|  | Total Due | $ 334.05 |

### Family Package

| Qty | Item | Price |
|---|---|---|
| 8 | ONE Books | $ 240.00 |
| 100 | IPOP Stickers | 50.00 |
| 16 | Wristbands | 56.00 |
| 16 | Karma Coins | 80.00 |
| 8 | PAK Pins | 80.00 |
| 8 | QLA Pins | 80.00 |
| 8 | WAM! Mugs | 200.00 |
|  | Subtotal | $ 786.00 |
|  | 20% Discount | 157.20 |
|  | Total Due | $ 628.80 |

### Friends Package

| Qty | Item | Price |
|---|---|---|
| 12 | ONE Books | $ 360.00 |
| 150 | IPOP Stickers | 75.00 |
| 24 | Wristbands | 84.00 |
| 24 | Karma Coins | 120.00 |
| 12 | PAK Pins | 120.00 |
| 12 | QLA Pins | 120.00 |
| 12 | WAM! Mugs | 300.00 |
|  | Subtotal | $ 1,179.00 |
|  | 25% Discount | 294.75 |
|  | Total Due | $ 884.25 |

### Holiday Gift Package

| Qty | Item | Price |
|---|---|---|
| 16 | ONE Books | $ 480.00 |
| 200 | IPOP Stickers | 100.00 |
| 32 | Wristbands | 112.00 |
| 32 | Karma Coins | 160.00 |
| 16 | PAK Pins | 160.00 |
| 16 | QLA Pins | 160.00 |
| 16 | WAM! Mugs | 400.00 |
|  | Subtotal | $ 1,572.00 |
|  | 30% Discount | 471.60 |
|  | Total Due | $ 1,100.40 |
|  | Name on Cover | Additional |
|  | Book Intro Page | $ 475.00 |

### Team Package

| Qty | Item | Price |
|---|---|---|
| 30 | ONE Books | $ 900.00 |
| 500 | IPOP Stickers | 250.00 |
| 60 | Wristbands | 210.00 |
| 60 | Karma Coins | 300.00 |
| 30 | PAK Pins | 300.00 |
| 30 | QLA Pins | 300.00 |
| 30 | WAM! Mugs | 750.00 |
|  | Subtotal | $ 3,010.00 |
|  | 35% Discount | 1,053.50 |
|  | Total Due | $ 1,956.50 |
|  | Name on Cover | Additional |
|  | Book Intro Page | $ 475.00 |

**Order on PAK App**

Get PAK App

**For Larger Custom Orders Please Call 212.213.0257 or Contact Us on App**

# BOOK BUYING & BRANDING

## SPONSORSHIP GUIDE FOR INDIVIDUALS, ORGS, GOVERNMENT & COMPANIES

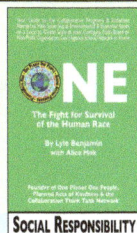

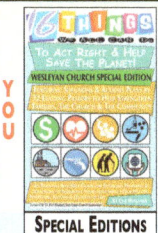

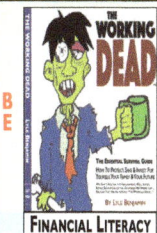

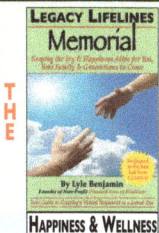

| SOCIAL RESPONSIBILITY | 16 THINGS ... | CUSTOMIZED ... | SPECIAL EDITIONS | FINANCIAL LITERACY | HAPPINESS & WELLNESS |
|---|---|---|---|---|---|

### NETWORKING • PR • FUND-RAISING • CSR • SUSTAINABILITY • ROI • RECRUITING & RETAINMENT • HR • BENEFITS

| UNBRANDED DISCOUNTED BULK ORDERS | PACKAGES FROM 25 BOOKS UP TO 100,000 | BRANDING STARTS AT 250 BOOKS | GREAT FOR CSR, BUSINESS DEVELOPMENT | SHAREHOLDERS & STAKEHOLDERS | COLLABORATIONS ADD TO YOUR BOTTOM LINE |
|---|---|---|---|---|---|

### NO WHERE WILL YOU FIND MORE MEANINGFUL WAYS TO CONNECT TO SO MANY WITH SUCH AN INSPIRATIONAL IMPACT

| BOOK QUANTITY | 250 | 500 | 1,000 | 2,500 | 5,000 | 10,000 | 25,000 | 50,000 | 100,000 |
|---|---|---|---|---|---|---|---|---|---|
| NAME ON COVER | YES | YES | YES | YES | YES | YES | YES | YES | YES |
| FOREWORD | 1 PAGE | 1 PAGE | 1 PAGE | 1 PAGE | 1 PAGE | 1 PAGE | 1 PAGE | 1 PAGE | 1 PAGE |
| MISSION | HALF PAGE | HALF PAGE | HALF PAGE | 1 PAGE | 1 PAGE | 2 PAGES | 2 PAGES | 2 PAGES | 2 PAGES |
| CHAPTER | HALF PAGE | HALF PAGE | HALF PAGE | 1 PAGE | 1 PAGE | 2 PAGES | 3 PAGES | 5 PAGES | 8 PAGES |
| DISPLAY PAGE(S) | NO | NO | 1 PAGE 4C | 2 PAGE SPREAD | 2 PAGE SPREAD | 2 PAGE SPREAD | 4 PAGE SPREAD | 6 PAGE SPREAD | 8 PAGE SPREAD |
| CEO BIOGRAPHY | HALF PAGE | HALF PAGE | HALF PAGE | 1 PAGE | 1 PAGE | 2 PAGES | 3 PAGES | 3 PAGES | 4 PAGES |
| OPT-IN PROGRAMS | LEVEL 1 | LEVEL 2 | LEVEL 2 | LEVEL 2 | LEVEL 3 | LEVEL 3 | LEVEL 4 | LEVEL 4 | LEVEL 5 |
| SPLIT RUNS | NO | NO | NO | NO | NO | NO | 2: 10K MIN. | 3: 15K MIN. | 4: 20K MIN. |
| BOOK PRICE UNBRANDED | $ 7,500 | $ 15,000 | $ 30,000 | $ 75,000 | $ 150,000 | $ 300,000 | $ 750,000 | $ 1,500,000 | $ 3,000,000 |
| DISCOUNT PERCENTAGE | 17% | 20% | 23% | 27% | 30% | 35% | 40% | 45% | 50% |
| PER UNIT DISCOUNT | 5.00 | 6.00 | 7.00 | 8.00 | 9.00 | 10.50 | 12.00 | 13.50 | 15.00 |
| TOTAL BOOK DISCOUNT | 1,250 | 3,000 | 7,000 | 20,000 | 45,000 | 105,000 | 300,000 | 675,000 | 1,500,000 |
| AMOUNT DUE | $ 6,250 | $ 12,000 | $ 23,000 | $ 55,000 | $ 105,000 | $ 195,000 | $ 450,000 | $ 825,000 | $ 1,500,000 |
| TOTAL PACKAGE VALUE | $ 68,500 | $ 151,500 | $ 312,000 | $ 839,875 | $1,767,000 | $ 3,716,000 | $10,500,000 | $ 25,440,000 | $57,000,000 |
| OR BASE FUNDRAISING AMOUNT | | | | | | | | | |

| OPT-IN PROGRAMS | LEVEL 1 | LEVEL 2 | LEVEL 3 | LEVEL 4 | LEVEL 5 |
|---|---|---|---|---|---|
| LISTING IN PAK APP | YES | YES | YES | YES | YES |
| PRODUCTS SOLD IN PAK SHOPPING CART | YES | YES | YES | YES | YES |
| SOCIAL MEDIA PROMOTION | YES | YES | YES | YES | YES |
| POP WORKSHOP BRANDING | YES | YES | YES | YES | YES |
| 6THINGS BOOK BASED WORKSHOP BRANDING | 500 | 2,000 | 5,000 | 10,000 | 20,000 |
| CUSTOM BENEFITS PROGRAM | — | YES | YES | YES | YES |
| EMPLOYEE VOLUNTEER PROGRAM | — | YES | YES | YES | YES |
| PRESS RELEASE INCLUSION | — | — | YES | YES | YES |
| CEO/PRESIDENT INTERVIEWED BY FOUNDER | — | — | YES | YES | YES |
| FOUNDER AS SPEAKER AT EVENT | — | — | YES | YES | YES |
| BOARD OF ADVISORS POSITION | — | — | — | YES | YES |
| EXCLUSIVE PROJECT-LEVEL DEVELOPMENT WITH FOUNDER | — | — | — | YES | YES |
| FOUNDER MASTERMIND PROGRAM | — | — | — | — | YES |
| AFFILIATE DISCOUNT OR COMPENSATION ON PAID COURSES | 15% | 20% | 25% | 30% | 35% |
| AFFILIATE DISCOUNT OR COMPENSATION ON SELECT PAID PROGRAMS | 15% | 20% | 25% | 30% | 35% |
| DISCOUNT ON SELECT PAID TEAM BUILDING PROGRAM | 15% | 20% | 25% | 30% | 35% |

**Scan the QR Code**

**Visit The ONE Book #107**

107

# SOCIAL RESPONSIBILITY PRODUCT
# OUTREACH ENGAGEMENT GUIDE

PAK & ONE PLANET ONE PEOPLE ITEMS CAN BE PURCHASED THROUGH OUR APP.
ALL ITEMS CAN BE CUSTOMIZED FOR FUND-RAISERS OR JOINT PROMOTIONS.
CONTACT US IF YOU DON'T SEE WHAT YOU WANT/LIKE ~ WE CAN CREATE!

KINDNESS WRISTBANDS

KINDNESS CARDS

KINDNESS CUPS

KINDNESS PINS

KINDNESS COINS

TEE SHIRTS

BOOKS

# SECTION XII:
# MORE ABOUT US

"THE MEANING OF LIFE
IS TO FIND YOUR GIFT.
THE PURPOSE OF LIFE
IS TO GIVE IT AWAY."
— PABLO PICASSO

# MANAGEMENT TEAM

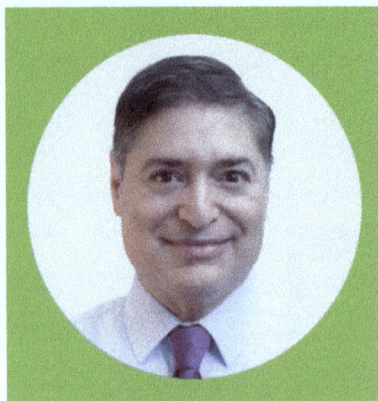

**Lyle Benjamin**
Systems / Writing / Design
New York NY

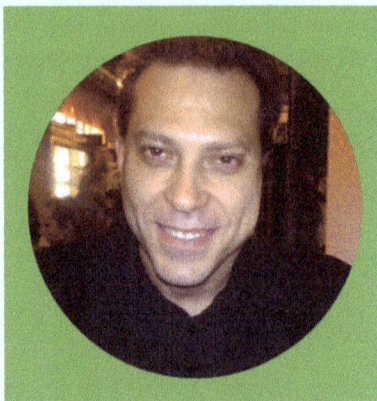

**Robert Adamo**
Operations / IT / Marketing
North Bergen NJ

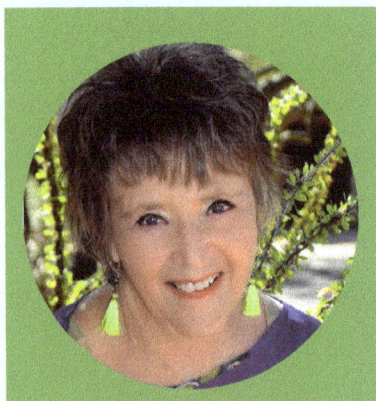

**Jacque Zoccoli**
Global Engagement
Tempe AZ

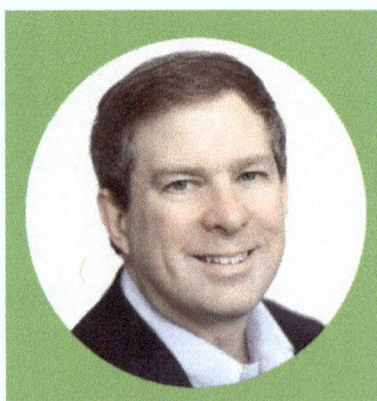

**Bill Harrison**
Publicity & Audience Building
Philadelphia PA

**Antuan Powell**
Social Media Engagement
Los Angeles CA

**Amy Collins**
Book Publishing & Marketing
Rochester NY

# LYLE BENJAMIN · BIOGRAPHY

NOVA'S OFFERS
HIS OPINION

When Benjamin was growing up, he had a difficult family life. Born three months premature and weighing only two pounds and three ounces, he spent months in a hospital incubator. After his parents divorced when he was seven, Benjamin felt there was too much discord between his four siblings and at eleven years old he decided to live with his father in New York City.

That same year, he went out on his own and landed a job working doing floral decoration, customer service and deliveries for a neighborhood florist. While working he met other store owners and managers that took an interest in him, and helped him deal with a difficult home life, just by talking and listening.

Then after moving to a new city in South Florida in the middle of his junior year in High School, Benjamin was given an IQ test and placed in the "gifted" program. Despite not learning to read until he was in 3rd grade, he now discovered a love for high level literary analysis and writing.

Now after doing very well in school, his parents had him finish high school six months early so he could work to earn money for college. Two days later, Benjamin got a job in the largest bookstore in South Florida where he worked an average of 63 hours a week and eventually became floor manager in charge of book and magazine ordering.

Over the years, Benjamin encountered many people that befriended him — from friend's parents, teachers and places he worked as a teen-ager. He grew to realize that these people were really a life saver for him, and he appreciated their acts of kindness so much that he wanted to become an attorney and devote his life helping others because of the kindness that he was shown.

After going to law school and being offered a job with the Attorney General's Office in Albany, New York, Benjamin decided the profession was not ideally suited for his goals of helping people.

Benjamin then turned his sideline business of resume and report writing and production into a typesetting, printing and design business. It was there that he honed the design and marketing skills that would serve him so well in business.

Never forgetting his obligation to help others, Benjamin created a prototype for a national self-help magazine. He sold his printing business in Gainesville and moved to New York City where he pitched it to Time Warner and Kable News. Both companies offered him contracts, and six months later he published "Relationships Today" the first national newsstand magazine exclusively devoted to helping people with all types of relationship issues: intimate, family, friendship and work.

Benjamin also created the best-selling board game "Romantic Journey" that helped tens of thousands of people enjoy better intimacy and communication in their relationships — making him the only person in the country ever to have created and published both a national magazine and best-selling board game at the same time.

Although the magazine was very well received by readers and the psychological community, it required too deep pockets over the long haul. After working 110-hour weeks Benjamin took to a break from New York life, moved to Albuquerque, New Mexico and focused on his writing.

A year later, Benjamin finished his first novel, secured Peter Miller, a very well-known literacy agent, and had moved back to New York. But once there, a friend needed Benjamin's help, and much to displeasure of his agent, he spent nine months turning around a struggling publication company that was going to fold after 14 years in business.

Benjamin's next entrepreneurial venture was the creation of Locations, Etc., a meeting and event planning business that scouted, coordinated and managed corporate and social events including workshops and conferences, fund-raisers, fashion shows, product launches, receptions, and holiday parties. To gain exposure and clients, Benjamin published "The Locations, Etc. Directory," an 8.5" x 11" 256-page black and white, and full color reference book on facilities and services that was sold at Barnes & Noble and other outlets.

It was during this time that Benjamin married and had two boys, Eric and Ryan. Because of their outgoing personalities, Benjamin thought his boys might enjoy modeling and acting, so he put together a marketing kit and contact several New York agencies. From there, his sons were signed up and sent out to auditions. Eric, the oldest, landed numerous modeling jobs with companies including Phat Farm, Toys R Us and Macy's, and publications including Parents and Scholastic.

When Benjamin thought the time was right, he secured a second agency to rep his boys for acting and they went on to do television appearances on everything from commercials to tv shows including "Blues Clues."

The highlight came after Eric auditioned and was cast in his first major motion picture, the Warner Brothers production of "The Invasion" starring Nicole Kidman and Daniel Craig. The production was spread out over six months between Baltimore and California and during that Benjamin and his son wrote about their experiences. Their journal became a book about the acting industry entitled "My Movie with Nicole Kidman" published by Seven Locks Press.

Both boys did well-enough in the industry to earn their SAG (Screen Actors Guild) union cards, something that most adult actors spend years working towards but never achieving.

Over the years, Benjamin also helped his wife move up the corporate ladder and become an award-winner Senior Creative Designer and Vice-President with multi-national companies including AECOM and JP Morgan Chase.

But Benjamin felt that he was straying too far from his mission of giving back. So, in 2015, Benjamin founded "16 Things Kids Can Do," a non-profit educational organization that works for the betterment of kids, people, and the planet through a series of books, workshops, programs, and activities all designed to help people lead happier, healthier, and more successful lives.

Benjamin and his wife amicably divorced in 2016 over creative differences.

In 2019, Benjamin launched his most ambitious program ever, the non-profit organization "Planned Acts of Kindness" — a Global Social Responsibility Platform where people all over the world wake up and on their cell phones, computers and devices, there is a new daily Planned Act of Kindness that they can do with their family, friends, co-workers and in their community.

Unfortunately the Pandemic hit in March 2020, effectively killing all the program initiatives for the next two years. Benjamin himself contracted COVID-19 in March of 2020 and suffers from severe headaches 24/7 to this day.

In 2021 Benjamin expanded his One Planet One People movement into its own 501(c)3 Non-Profit Organization with a series of global programs and initiatives.

The goal these organizations is to help people obtain better Quality of Life, regardless of their country of origin, race, gender, age, religion, health, education or income.

Benjamin has two sons, a large cat named Nova, and a whole bunch of siblings.

# LYLE'S PERSONAL NOTES

Despite being dyslexic, Benjamin was an avid competitive Scrabble player who occasionally beat top 20 players in the world. He won three tournaments over his brief two-and-a-half year competitive career. His biggest disappointment was losing to the number one player in the world on the last turn of the game when he bingoed out to claim the 50 extra bonus points and win by 22 points.

His favorite sport is table tennis (ping pong) and has played Russians in Russia and Chinese in China earning much respect from opponents since he was neither Russian or Chinese.

His first (and only) sci-fi novel was written for Star Trek: The Next Generation. Entitled "A Not So Delicate Balance" it was a sociological story of racial enslavement set on an undersea world. It was accepted for publication by Bantam Books with the caveat of adding a sub-plot to boost the page count to meet their minimum hard-back publishing requirements — something Benjamin will do after he retires.

Benjamin loves to cook for family and friends and alledgedly is decent enough to have gotten requests to start his own restaurant. Having had restaurant owners as clients and friends in his printing and special events company, Benjamin swears that owning a restaurant is one of the top things he will never, ever do in business.

A comedic movie script he wrote based on a couple playing his game, "Romantic Journey" was offered a production contract by Video Corporation of America, but Benjamin turned it down because of the contract terms — something he may do after he retires.

P.S. Benjamin never plans on retiring from his Mission. But is up for an occasional game of Scrabble or ping pong!

P.S.S. 10+ years into this journey, Nova is still very much interested and engaged ... besides, who doesn't love a great cat picture!

# ALICE MOK · BIOGRAPHY

Alice Mok is an award-winning interior architect known to infuse her artistic sensibilities and ethos for corporations-driven projects. Her ingenious use of materials, bespoke designs and visionary sensibilities have set her apart as one of the leading interior architects of her generation.

During her university education at Melbourne RMIT she began to think about designing facilities that would provide better care for people, a moment she describes as changing everything. She came to the understanding that interior architecture should serve people and as a prevalent force within all our lives it too should take to the realm of egalitarianism. Alice has over 25 years of experience in Interior architectural and Environmental sustainability as practitioner.

After years of working in other architectural firms, she opened her own design studio in 2006. Since then, she has completed projects that are sensitive to the specific circumstances of sites while skillfully and imaginatively resolving complex design issues.

Alice acts as the Lead Interior Architect working on key relocation/renovation projects throughout the world with leading law firms, financial institutions, and multinational corporations. Her progressive career is a combination of facility planning, interior design and project management expertise. She provides overall leadership and technical direction for client teams, her design and construction teams, as well as for 3rd party project managers and in doing so, ensuring the incorporation of best practices in sustainability and building designs.

**Education:** Bachelor's Degree, First Class Honours, Interior & Environmental Design, RMIT University, Melbourne

**Awards:**
- Interior Design Award, Corporate Office Project from the Perspective Design Recognition in 2005, 2007
- Award, Asia Pacific Interior Design Association (APIDA) in 2003, 2006, 2013
- Interior Design Award, Corporate Office Project from Greater China Region Recognition in 2013, 2015

## Partial Client List:

MICROSOFT HEADQUARTERS SHANGHAI

- Apple
- Bank of China (Int'l.)
- BASF
- Bausch & Lomb
- BP - British Petroleum
- British American Tobacco
- Brown Brothers Harriman
- Calvin Klein
- CIGNA
- Carrefour
- Daiwa Securities SMBC
- Deloitte
- Egon Zehnder
- Exxon Mobile
- FOSSIL
- Franklin Templeton
- Fuji Xerox
- General Electric
- Gucci
- Hang Seng Bank
- Hitachi
- ING Insurance
- Invesco
- MasterCard
- Mayer-Brown JSM
- McKinsey & Co.
- Nokia
- Nvidia
- Procter & Gamble
- SF Express
- Shell Oil
- Siemens
- Sony Pictures
- Sumitomo Corp.
- Sun Hung Kai
- Tiffany & Co.

# THE JOURNEY BEGINS...

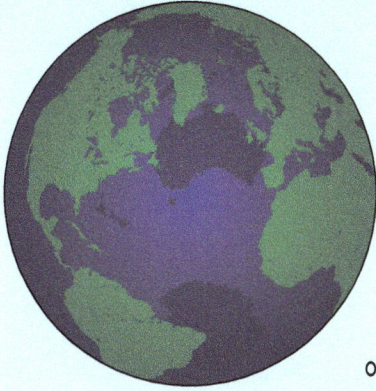

The road ahead is a difficult one. The challenges to humanity I've detailed in the **ONE** book are astronomically large and mind-bogglingly complex. But if we could collectively come together and accomplish one of the greatest feats of the Human Race — getting people safely to the moon and back using nothing more powerful than today's discount cell phone — I believe we can come together and conquer the social, environmental, and economic issues that threaten our quality of life on this planet.

On September 12, 1962, with one momentous statement, U.S. President John F. Kennedy forever changed the trajectory of the world. "We choose to go to the moon in this decade and do the other things, not because they are easy, but because they are hard."

Let us honor that bold action by launching the programs and initiatives that make up the foundation for One Planet One People and Quality of Life for all.

On September 12, 2022, sixty years later, let's make the commitment to have our E-QL Kindness in Education and our One Planet One People Social Responsibility Youth Clubs in schools in all 200 countries around the world. Let's have our Work/Life Balance CSR/HR Programs available for employees, contractors, and families through schools, non-profits, government agencies, and businesses. And most importantly, when striving to achieve the same objectives, let's end the fractional approach that divides us.

For the handful of people on the planet that control more wealth than 90% of all the people in the world, it's time for them to step up and give back. Do it for your family, your country, your global community, your legacy, but do it before it's too late.

If JFK were alive today and witnessed three people paying a collective $165 million to go into space, what would he say about our progress after all these years? I believe he would be deeply saddened to see how far we come with our technology, while our Quality of Life issues are still mired in the 1970s.

I believe that this is the time for humanity to rise to the occasion and accept the responsibility of another heroic challenge: "As One Planet One People, we choose to turn back the tipping points issues that threaten Quality of Life on our planet in this decade and do the other things, not because they are easy, but because they are necessary for our humanity."

In this spirit, let us challenge ourselves and those around us — the rich, the poor, the busy, the passive — to get involved and take action, and "Be The Heroes" that the world so desperately needs.

Let us, before this opportunity passes and this decade comes to a close, echo the astounding success of an earlier time, "Houston, Tranquility Base here. The Eagle has landed."

Let us live up to the ideals of humanity, and only then may we truly "Live Long and Prosper."

115

# Afterword

"You may say I'm a dreamer
But I'm not the only one
I hope someday you'll join us
And the world will be as one
— John Lennon

I am a dreamer. Throughout my life I normally sleep only five to six hours a night. In March of 2021, I got Covid-19 and experienced loss of taste and smell, and chills and fatigue for three weeks. I slept 10 to 14 hours a day and couldn't work. I had no fever or respiratory issues whatsoever. After three weeks my chills and fatigue ended, replaced by crushing headaches 24/7. Headaches that varied in pain from 3-4 out of 10 at its lowest to 7 and 8 where all I could do was curl up and cry.

But despite my headaches I still dreamt. Despite the cancellation to the planned launch of three education and action books, and my non-profit Planned Acts of Kindness, I still dreamt and worked when I felt well enough. And that worked out to about 20% of my normal productivity.

My sleep patterns, which was never quite what others thought they should be, went from working during the day, evening and into the early morning to almost exclusively working from midnight to 4, 5, 6, 7 and 8 in the morning. If I felt well enough to work at these times, then work I would. And I did.

The doctors and neurologists I saw put me through a variety of drug therapies including an escalating cocktail of injectables … none of which really worked for me. When all else fails, the last line of treatment is Botox. 30 injections into my scalp, face, neck, and shoulders every three months.

At the beginning of the year, nine months into my headaches, I started to notice that I could work for longer periods of time and get started earlier in the day. I was ecstatic. Maybe I was finally getting a handle on this thing. It was only the lull before the storm. My third Botox treatment came and went, and I'm still waiting for it to do its magic.

But I am still a dreamer and I'm not the only one.
I hope today you'll join us and soon the world will be as one.